Muslim and Christian Reflections on Peace

Divine and Human Dimensions

Edited by
J. Dudley Woodberry
Osman Zümrüt
Mustafa Köylü

UNIVERSITY PRESS OF AMERICA,® INC.
Lanham • Boulder • New York • Toronto • Oxford

Copyright © 2005 by
University Press of America,® Inc.
4501 Forbes Boulevard
Suite 200
Lanham, Maryland 20706
UPA Acquisitions Department (301) 459-3366

PO Box 317
Oxford
OX2 9RU, UK

Library of Congress Control Number: 2004115712
ISBN 0-7618-2998-9 (paperback : alk. ppr.)

Contents

Preface

When Muslim and Christian scholars met in Samsun, Turkey, for a symposium on inter-religious dialogue as a contribution to world peace, little did we know that September 11 was less than three months away. The events of that tragic day underline the urgency of such dialogue. As conflicts surfaced in Afghanistan, Palestine/Israel, Kashmir, Pakistan, Chechnya, and Iraq, the need was evident for our communities to discuss underlying issues and not just military responses.

On the way to Samsun, we expatriate scholars visited the Topkapi Palace, passing through the Gate of Peace (Bab al-Salam) and prayed that somehow this symposium might be a step in that direction. We also visited the Hagia Sophia, which has housed both Christian and Muslim worship. As we looked up into the dome, we read the qur'anic words "God is the light of the heavens and earth" (al-Nur [24]:35), and we wondered what our Muslim counterparts would offer from the Qur'an from Him who is called therein "All-peaceable" (al-Hashr [59]:23). At the same time we knew that beneath those words was an earlier representation of the head of Jesus in whom Christians saw "the light of the knowledge of the glory of God in the face of Jesus Christ" (2 Corinthians 4:6), and we reflected on what we might share from him whom Christians call the Prince of Peace (Isa. 9:6).

The dialogue was held in Samsun, the birthplace of the revolution, which in 1923 declared Turkey a secular state, hence set a Muslim-majority nation on a course with the potential for Muslims and Christians to share as equals. Yet the challenges were formidable in a setting which had experienced the ravages of the Crusades and the conquest of Constantinople. Both Islam and

Christianity are missionary religions with a message for all people (al-Furqan [25]:1; Sad [38]:87; Al 'Imran [3]:20; John 3:16.) They each claim the final messenger (al-Ahzab [33]:40; Hebrews 1:1-2) and make exclusive claims for their message (Al 'Imran [3]:85; John 14:6; Acts 4:12). Both groups of followers are to be witnesses (al-Baqara [2]:143; Matthew 28:19-20; Acts 1:8). Yet each is to witness in a respectful way:

> Invite to the way of your Lord with wisdom and good exhortation (Surah al-Nahl [16]:125).

> Dispute not with the People of the Book except in the best way (Surah al-'Ankabut [29]:46).

> Always be prepared to give an answer to anyone who calls you to account for the hope that is in you with gentleness and respect (1 Peter 3:15).

The symposium was opened with welcoming addresses by the President of Religious Affairs of Turkey Mehmet Nuri Yilmaz, the Governor of the Province of Samsun Muammer Güler, the Mayor of the city of Samsun Yusuf Ziya Yilmaz, the Rector of Ondokuz Mayis University Ferit Bernay, and the Dean of its Faculty of Theology Osman Zümrüt. On behalf the guests David E. Wong of Professional and Educational Services International (P.E.S.I.) told of his beneficial experience of living as a Christian in Samsun, which led to the idea for such a symposium. Kenneth Chin, President of P.E.S.I. which arranged for the guest contingent to attend the symposium, used the saying of Confucius "Within the four seas all people are brothers [and sisters]" as a theme to relate how such interchanges had been helpful in China and hoped that the same would be true in Turkey.

The Christian contribution to the papers included in this volume is introduced by Miroslav Volf, Henry B. Wright Professor of Theology at Yale University Divinity School. In his paper "Living with the 'Other'" he explores, in a context of people from different religious traditions, how we can embrace even as we argue about truth and justice, and he notes the special contributions such as grace that Christians can add to the discussion.

Dudley Woodberry, Professor of Islamic Studies at Fuller Theological Seminary, in his paper "Toward Common Ground in Understanding the Human Condition" points out how the root of world conflicts is the human condition. Muslims have traditionally looked at humans as born with a good or neutral human nature, hence only needing right guidance. The biblical picture, however, is of humans who, though made in the image of God, are fallen. As a result they need more than right guidance; they need God's spirit resulting in a new birth. A closer look at the Qur'an, however, suggests a diagnosis of the human condition that is closer to the biblical one than is normally understood. Hence it implies that the necessary solution may be closer too.

Christians understand the crucifixion and resurrection of Jesus as being a means by which God forgives humans and gives them new life, but most Muslims believe that they are denied by the Qur'an. Joseph Cumming, a Fellow of Yale University, however, notes that a number of the most authoritative Muslim commentators on the Qur'an allow for a real crucifixion and resurrection as a legitimate interpretation of the qur'anic materials. Thus the crucifixion need not be as big a problem for Muslims in their understanding of the solution to human sin.

Since peace requires more than a correct analysis of the human condition, and forgiveness and new life for individuals, Ng Kam Weng, Director of the Kairos Research Centre in Kuala Lumpur, Malaysia, presents a paper on "Covenant Community in a Divided World." Here he shows how the Bible presents a way of life that is centered in love and obedience to God and a community that can heal the divisions in our world.

Finally, Jonathan E. Culver, Professor of Theology at Tyranus Biblical Seminary in Bandung, Indonesia, takes a topic that has been a source of considerable misunderstanding between Muslims and Christians. In his paper "The Ishmael Promises: A Bridge for Mutual Respect," he begins to build that bridge.

The Muslim contributions by faculty and one graduate student of Ondokuz Mayis University are divided between those that deal with broad general issues and those that deal with narrower topics. First, Dean Osman Zümrüt, Professor of the History of Islam, in "The Contribution of Religions to World Peace" points out that a contribution to peace of world religions is their emphasis on such values as the fundamental unity of the human family and the equality and dignity of all human beings. Then he identifies what he considers to be special contributions of Islam. Mahmut Aydin, Associate Professor of the History of Religions and Inter-religious Dialogue, looks at the context of dialogue in "Religious Pluralism as an Opportunity for Living Together in Diversity." He sees the claims of world religions to absolute truth as a major challenge and religious pluralism as a major opportunity for people of different religions to learn to live together.

In "A Common Human Agenda for Christians and Muslims," Mustafa Köylü, Assistant Professor of Religious Education, argues that there are limits to theological dialogue. Priority instead should be given to living our faith in the common service of humanity, thereby working against oppression and poverty. In "An Islamic Approach toward International Peace" Israfil Balci, a doctoral student of the history of Islam, notes the more peaceful flavor of the

earlier Meccan suras of the Qur'an as opposed to the increasingly militant flavor in the later Medinan period. He argues against those that say that the latter position abrogates the former, by asserting that it is the attitude of the non-
Muslims that determines the response of the Qur'an. Therefore, Islam along
with the other religions provide roots of peace and justice for the world.

The final three chapters deal with issues that contribute toward world
peace. Sinasi Gündüz, Assistant Professor of the History of Religions, in his
paper "Hegemonic Power Versus *tawhīd*: A Decisive Concept of Islam on Interfaith Relations" notes how in history hegemonic power has often been the
major influence in encounters between religions. In contrast to this and the
pluralistic view that all religions are different routes to salvation, he argues
that the Islamic doctrine of *tawhīd* should be the basic criterion of truth and
reality. It is a doctrine which emphasizes God's unity, uniqueness, and superiority, without associates; and the science of *tawhīd* contains all the other
branches of knowledge.

In "Wisdom as an Inter-Religious Concept for Peace" Cafer Sadik Yaran
says that the concept and value of wisdom is shared by religion, philosophy
and science. Furthermore, Islam does not restrict it to the Qur'an and the traditions of Muhammad, and it has the quality of peacefulness. Therefore, it
forms a natural subject for dialogue toward peace. Burhanettin Tatar in
"Some Remarks on the Authority of Sacred Texts and Violence" shows ways
in which religious communities exercise violence on sacred texts or use them
to legitimate violence. He argues for a position in which "the authority of sacred texts can lead its followers to produce something good by strengthening
mutual understanding both among themselves and with people of other
faiths." This, it would seem, would allow for others to contribute their insights as to how each community might interpret its sacred scriptures.

Many helped to make this English collection of papers possible—the Theological Faculty of Ondokuz Mayis University for hosting the consultation,
Professional and Educational Services International for providing travel for
expatriate participants, and Margie Waldo and Robin Basselin for painstaking
editorial work. This publication was supported by Award No. 2003-DD-BX-
1025 awarded by the U.S. Department of Justice, Office of Justice Programs.
The opinions, findings, and conclusions or recommendations expressed in
this publication are those of the authors and do not necessarily reflect the
views of the Department of Justice.

These papers—some complementary, others contrasting—are attempts by
the individual authors to further peace—both with God and each other. The
traditional Muslim greeting "Peace" (*salam*) conveys the wholeness of this
concept which includes both the physical and the spiritual. The Apostle Paul
in writing to people living in what is now Turkey took the greeting of the East

"Peace" (*shalom/salam*) and added the greeting of the West "Grace" (*charis*). The latter word was used in the Greek translation of the Hebrew scriptures to express the lovingkindness of God for those who did not deserve it and in the New Testament for the forgiveness and love of God in Jesus the Messiah. What better place is there than Turkey, which straddles East and West, to combine these concepts again? For true peace will never be realized without forgiveness and love.

Grace and peace,
J. Dudley Woodberry

The Context For Reflection

Distinguished governmental and educational leaders put the following reflections in context at a dialogue on June 19–20, 2001, at the School of Divinity at the Ondokuz Mayis University in Samsun, Turkey, where Mustafa Kemal Atatürk and fellow officers started their War of Independence. Included here are excerpts.

VARIETY OF RELIGIONS BY DIVINE INTENT, BY MEHMET NURI YILMAZ, TURKISH MINISTER OF RELIGIOUS AFFAIRS

In order to remove the prejudices and walls that have built up between religions and cultures, we must establish an environment that allows for reciprocal dialogue. We should always remember our responsibility to learn from history and avoid the mistakes of the past. Throughout history, religious conflicts have been the source of wars, conflicts, tragedies, and the destruction of sacred places. To avoid repeating this, it is necessary that all People of the Book pursue genuine understanding and dialogue with one another.

Islam accepts the variety of religions and belief systems in the world. In a sense, they exist by divine intention, and consequently, we are forced to live together and deal with one another. Our sacred book, The Qur'an, accepts the existence of various religions and beliefs and consequently sees religious pluralism as consistent with the will and wisdom of God. It says: *"To each among you have We prescribed a law an open way. If Allah had so willed, He would have made you a single people, but [His plan is] to test you in what He hath given you; so strive as in a race in all virtues. The goal of you all is to Allah; It is He that will show you the truth of the matters in which ye dispute"* (al-Ma'ida [5]:48).

Various cultures and civilizations in the world exist because Allah has preferred the created order to be full of diversity. Allah says in al-Hujurat [49]:13, *"O mankind! We created you from a single [pair] of a male and a female, and made you into nations and tribes, that ye may know each other. . . ."* This emphasizes that a variety of religions and cultures, in other words religious pluralism, is intended to be a source of richness and happiness to human beings.

There will certainly be theological discussion and debate between religions. Just as in the past, these will continue in our day. These discussions will further our academic knowledge, but more importantly they will also help each of us in our understanding of Allah and His message to humankind. This will open up the way for every religion to study itself in universal and systematic terms. Accordingly, every religion will feel the need to be ready for this type of interaction. To me, it is not the presence, but the absence or inadequacy of healthy debate that will have serious negative consequences. Therefore, debate should not be seen as an obstacle to genuine dialogue. We should always keep in mind that at the end of many of the verses concerning relations between religions, Almighty God emphasizes that ultimate knowledge belongs to Him alone.

SAMSUN: THE BIRTHPLACE OF INDEPENDENCE, BY MUANNER GÜLER, GOVERNOR OF ISTANBUL AND FORMER GOVERNOR OF SAMSUN

Samsun is where the foundations of the Republic of Turkey were laid. Here the Turkish nation took its first steps toward independence. And now in this same city, the Ondokuz Mayis University and its School of Divinity, while guarding the principles and reforms of Atatürk are taking steps to address the difficulties raised by religion at an international level. We see this symposium as a first step toward this aim.

THE IMPORTANCE OF UNDERSTANDING, BY FERIT BERNAY, RECTOR, ONDOKUZ MAYIS UNIVERSITY

I hope that this symposium will contribute important things. First, it will serve to overcome the stereotypes, bias, ignorance, misunderstanding, misinformation, and caricatures existing between Muslims and Christians. Second, since dialogue is two-ways, both sides will have a chance to learn about each other and act accordingly. Third, these kinds of activities will not only contribute toward a more accurate understanding of religious matters, but also contribute toward world peace and religious freedom for all, religious and nonreligious alike.

FIRST PRESIDENT: "PEACE AT HOME; PEACE ABROAD," BY OSMAN ZÜMRÜT, DEAN, SCHOOL OF DIVINITY, ONDOKUZ MAYIS UNIVERSITY

With today's symposium, the School of Theology has taken a first step toward a goal given to us by Atatürk. Citizens of Samsun, it is here that the Turkish War of Independence began. Today, we will discuss the principles of world peace, which Atatürk summarized many years ago when he said, "Peace at home, peace abroad." Focusing on this issue, our academicians are presenting various views on the topic.

WHERE EAST AND WEST MEET, BY KENNETH P. CHIN, PRESIDENT, PROFESSIONAL AND EDUCATIONAL SERVICES, INTERNATIONAL

"Within the four seas, all men are brothers." This Chinese proverb describes the ideal for a world where there is peace and harmony among all people. It is certainly with this spirit that we have come together. I represent a group of Chinese American professionals who promote international development. With our dual cultural heritage as Asians and Americans, we believe that it is both our privilege and responsibility to serve as a bridge between East and West.

When David Wong was our representative here in Samsun, he experienced how this nation, straddling Europe and Asia, is uniquely positioned to serve as a bridge not only between East and West, but also between Muslims and Christians. It is our sincere hope that mutual understanding will take place now and in the days ahead for *"within the four seas, all men are brothers."*

Part One

CHRISTIAN REFLECTIONS

Chapter One

LIVING WITH THE "OTHER"[1]

Miroslav Volf
Henry B. Wright Professor of Theology
Yale University Divinity School

INTRODUCTION: SPEAKING IN A CHRISTIAN VOICE

In a world where Christians and Muslims are ever-increasingly living amongst each other, it is important to examine what our traditions say about living with the other, and to highlight resources that they provide for overcoming enmities and living in peace. Since I am a Christian, I will speak in a Christian voice. Though I seek to be faithful to the broad Christian tradition, I cannot speak authoritatively for all Christians; nobody can, because ecclesiastically Christians are not a monolithic group and even within a single church there is often disagreement and spirited debate. So I offer here my rendering of what the Christian tradition says about "living with 'the other'." Before I continue, however, let me briefly indicate what I mean by speaking in a "Christian voice" in an interfaith context. A simple way to do so is to discard two wrongheaded options and then suggest a better one.

Some suggest that all major world religions are at the bottom more or less the same. What is significant in each is common to them all. What makes each differ from others is only a husk conditioned by various human mentalities but holding an identical kernel. In *An Interpretation of Religion*, John Hick comes close to this view in that, together with Jalalu'l-Din Rumi, he argues that "the lamps are different, but the Light is the same."[2] To speak in a Christian voice from the perspective of such an understanding of religion means to engage in cracking the husk of difference that distinguishes the Christian faith from other religions and displaying the kernel which unites it

3

with them. Whoever speaks authentically in a Christian voice will end up agreeing with representatives of other religions provided they do the same.

While all major religions have much in common, including some fundamental convictions, and while their adherents all possess the same human dignity and therefore command the same respect, it is not clear that all religions are at bottom the same. Most of their adherents would disagree with the claim and feel that the one making it does not sufficiently respect them in their own specificity but is, as it were, looking through them in search of an artificially constructed essence of their religion. My sense is that they are right. Major religions represent distinctive overarching interpretations of life with partly overlapping and partly competing metaphysical, historical, and moral claims. To treat all religions as at the bottom the same is to insert them into a frame of meaning without sufficiently appreciating, as Michael Barnes puts it in *Theology and the Dialogue of Religions*, "the irreducible mystery of otherness" of religions.[3] It is because all major religions are not at the bottom the same that it is worth engaging in dialogues; such dialogues are exercises in mutual learning about ourselves and others. Equally, it is because all major religions are not at the bottom the same that their adherents rightly argue with each other about the merits and truth content of their respective religions.

An alternative view agrees that major world religions represent distinct overarching interpretations of life, but goes on to suggest that what is important in each tradition are precisely the places where they differ. This view is rarely defended theoretically; it represents more an unreflective way of relating to other religions, a stance toward them. With such a stance, what matters the most, for instance, is not that the children of Abraham all believe in one God, but that Christians believe that this one God is a Holy Trinity whereas Jews and Muslims staunchly object to this claim. To speak in a Christian voice is to highlight what is specific to Christianity and leave out what is common as comparatively unimportant.

But concentrating on differences seems to be a major mistake, so basic that it includes a mistake about how to define something. As any introduction to logic will make clear, you cannot define an entity by noting only its specific difference; you must also include in your definition its proximate genus. Human beings are rational animals; "rational" is the specific difference and "animal" is the proximate genus. Applied to the world of religions, what is important about the Christian convictions about God is not simply that God is the Holy Trinity, but also that the Father of Jesus Christ is the God who called Abraham and delivered the Jews from slavery in Egypt, which is, from a Christian perspective, the God whom Muslims worship as Allah. Similarly what is important about the Christian sacred texts is not only that they contain the New Testament, but also that they contain what Christians call the Old Testament, which is originally a Jewish sacred text, and that there is a significant overlap between Christian and Muslim sacred texts. To think of one's own or of another religion simply in terms of its differences from one's own is to fail to respect it in its concreteness.

In fact, both of the above approaches are wrongheaded because *they abstract from the concrete character of religions*, the one by zeroing in on what is the same in all religions and the other by zeroing in on what is different. In this they miss precisely what is most important about a religion, which is *the particular configuration of its elements*, which may overlap with, differ from, or contradict some elements of other religions. For religions are embraced and practiced in no other way but in their concreteness. To speak in a Christian voice is then neither to give a variation on a theme common to all religions nor to make exclusively Christian claims in distinction from all other religions; it is to give voice to the Christian faith in its concreteness, whether what is said overlaps with, differs from, or contradicts what people speaking in a Jewish or Muslim voice are saying. Since truth matters and since a false pluralism of approving pats on the back is cheap and short-lived, we will rejoice over overlaps and engage others over differences and incompatibilities, so as to both learn from and teach others.

When I say something like, "The Christian faith has important resources to address this issue," I by no means want to imply that other religions do not have similar or even better resources. What I am doing is simply speaking in a Christian voice rather than offering a comparative analysis of religions. I hope that the content will either find resonance with my Jewish and Muslim hearers or that they will tell me, "Consider this from our tradition," or "But you got it all wrong, for these reasons." I take my comments to be part of a movement back and forth of all parties involved between engaged explication of their own religious tradition on the one hand, and receptive hearing of the explication of another tradition on the other.

My presentation has a simple outline. I will try to answer three questions: (1) Who is the "other"? (2) Who are we? (3) How should we relate to each other? I will then conclude with a brief reflection on the relation between the universal reach of Christian love (any and every person) and particular obligations toward those with whom we have special relations (such as our family, ethnic or religious group).

Before I proceed, let me make one linguistic observation. The title of my work uses the singular "other" with a definite article. This is how the word is often used in philosophical, sociological, and anthropological literature.[4] There is nothing wrong with such use, provided we are not misled by the singular to make two mistakes: either to think that the "other" is only of one kind, or to reduce all distinct features of others to an abstract otherness. First, "others" are many. They come in a variety of shapes and colors, speak diverse languages, espouse different religions, and are characterized by different cultural markers. The grammatical singular denotes a plural reality, which I will partly indicate by shifting back and forth between the singular and the plural. Second, otherness is not an abstract undifferentiated quality. Individual traits of others matter a great deal for how we relate to them. Others may be simply *different* from us (say, speak Hungarian instead of Croatian). Or we may *disapprove* of some of the constitutive features of their otherness (such as their use of alcohol or their practice of genital mutilation). Or the other may be someone who has *transgressed* against us (such as Hutus having massacred hundreds of thousands of Tutsis). Indeed, the other may be and often is all three of these things together. So "the other" is a shorthand which opens a window to a richly diverse reality, not the indicator of the full content of that reality.

WHO IS THE "OTHER"?

Some people think of others as persons from distant lands with a very different culture. We read about them in books written by explorers and anthropologists, we travel to see them in their natural habitats, they fascinate us and repel us at the same time, and we return from our imaginative or real excursions into their world to the familiarity and tranquility of our own homes. This is the *exotic* other. In our global culture, the exotic other has increasingly become a rarity. We travel with ease over vast expanses, and the mass media has placed at our disposal vivid reports even from the most hidden and impenetrable regions of the globe. It could seem that we have come to understand others much better. But this is by and large not the case, for a real understanding requires a deeper knowledge than is available through written reports, films or short visits. The ease of access to others has only stripped down from them the aura of the exotic. They have become ordinary — but still misunderstood.

The same communication networks that make it easy for us to meet and learn about distant others have brought multiple others to live in our immediate proximity. This is the *neighborly* other. Such others live next to us, at the boundaries of our communities and within our nations. Put differently, we live increasingly in culturally and religiously *pluralistic* social spaces. For Western countries, for instance, this means that the pluralism of civil associations existing under the larger framework of liberal democracy has been complexified. Formerly "Christian countries" have become religiously diverse nations.[5] But this is not a diversity of "anything goes." For the most part, we don't think that all religion and all values are either relative or that there is a rough parity between them. To say that our societies are culturally and religiously pluralistic is not so much to prescribe how each culture should be evaluated and how they should relate but to note that a plurality of cultures is a social reality. We live near or with people whose values and overarching interpretations of life differ markedly from ours and who have sufficient social power to make their voice heard in the public square. In terms of living with the other, the main challenge today is this rubbing shoulders with diverse people in an increasingly pluralistic world.

The history of relations with "the other" has often been fraught with violence. As the Holocaust survivor Primo Levi writes, "Many people—many nations—can find themselves holding, more or less wittingly, that 'every stranger is an enemy'."[6] Religious, cultural, and racial differences are an important source of conflicts around the world. We consider ourselves better on account of the color of our skin and put others, whose color is different from ours, down; we oppress them economically and marginalize them politically. Whites are well known for their sense of racial superiority. But racism is not a monopoly of the whites. A student friend of mine from Ethiopia who was a target of many racial slurs in the former Yugoslavia told me an Ethiopian story of creation:

> When God was creating man, God formed him out of the dust and put him in the oven to bake him. But he turned up the heat too high, so when he pulled the man out he was a bit too burned. This is how black people were created. Then God tried again, but this time he set the oven too low and out came the whites, which he couldn't do much with because they were under-baked. Then on the third attempt, the beautifully browned Ethiopians came out.

Ethiopians have no better opinion of the whites, my student suggested, than the whites of Ethiopians.

In recent years, cultural and ethnic clashes have left in their trail scorched land, rivers of blood, and mountains of corpses, in the so called Third World (e.g. Rwanda), in the former Second World (e.g. Chechnya or Bosnia) and in the First World (e.g. the Los Angeles riots). Then there are religious differences. Today, no less than in the past, conflicts rage around religious differences. Muslims and Christians, Christians and Jews, Jews and Muslims, Muslims and Hindus, Hindus and Buddhists are finding it difficult to share the same social space without conflicts, some of which have been extremely violent.

Though "otherness"—cultural, ethnic, religious, racial difference—is an important factor in our relations with others, we should not overestimate it as a cause of conflict. During the war in the former Yugoslavia in the early 1990s, I was often asked, "What is this war about? Is it about religious and cultural differences? Is it about economic advantage? Is it about political power? Is it about land?" The correct response was, of course, that the war was about all of these things. Mono-causal explanations of major eruptions of violence are rarely right. Moreover, various causes are intimately intertwined and each contributes to others. That holds true also for otherness. But neither should we underestimate otherness as a factor. The contest for political power, for economic advantage, and for the share of the land took place between people who belonged to discrete cultural and ethnic groups. And part of the goal of the war in the former Yugoslavia was the creation of ethnically clean territories with economic and political autonomy. The importance of "otherness" is only slightly diminished if we grant that the sense of ethnic and religious belonging was manipulated by unscrupulous, corrupt, and greedy politicians for the purposes of their own political and economic gain. The fact that conjured fears for one's identity could serve to legitimize a war whose major driving force lied elsewhere is itself a testimony to how much "otherness" matters.

Who are the others? They are people of different races, religions, and cultures, who live in our proximity and with whom we are often in tension and sometimes in deadly conflict. But who are we?

WHO ARE WE?

It is not possible to speak of "the other" without speaking of "the self," and of otherness without speaking of identity. For the others are always others to someone else, and just like that someone else they too are to themselves simply "us" as distinct from "them." But how should we think of ourselves? What does it mean to be a bearer of identity?

As I have already indicated in my preliminary remarks, we often define ourselves by what differentiates us from others. That by which we differ from others is properly and exclusively our own, and it is in what is exclusively our own that our identity resides, we sometimes think. If we operate with such an *exclusive* notion of identity, we will watch carefully to make sure that no external elements enter our proper space so as to disturb the purity of our identity. Especially in situations of economic and political uncertainty and conflict, we will insist on pure identity. If race matters to us, then we will want our "blood" to be pure, untainted by the "blood" of strangers. If land matters to us, then we will want our soil to be pure, without the presence of others. If culture matters to us, then we will want our language and customs to be pure, cleansed of foreign words and foreign ways. This is the *logic of purity*. It attends the notion of identity which rests on difference from the other. The consequences of the logic of purity in a pluralistic world are often deadly. We have to keep the other at bay, even by means of extreme violence, so as to avoid contamination.

An alternative way to construe identity is to think of it as always including the other. This is an *inclusive* understanding of identity. As persons or cultural groups, we define ourselves not simply by what distinguishes us from others and what we therefore need to keep pure from others. Instead, we define ourselves both by what distinguishes us from others and by what we have in common with them. This notion of identity is consonant with the Old Testament account of creation. In Genesis, God creates by separating things (say, the light from the darkness) and binding them together. When God creates a human pair, God both separates Eve from Adam and brings her to him so that they can become one flesh. Distinct-and-bound creatures necessarily have complex identities, because they are what they are, not just in and of themselves but also in relation to others.

Let me give you an example. Four years ago I became a father. I have a wonderful little boy, Nathanael. Now, after I became a father I remained the same person in the sense of having permanence and continuity over a period of time (what Paul Ricoeur calls *idem*-identity). But I did not remain the same person in the sense of my personality remaining unchanged (what Ricoeur calls *ipse*-identity).[7] Nathanael has insinuated himself into my personality. He has changed not only how I see myself and how I act (my private person) but also how others see me and act toward me (my public person). In addition to everything else that I was (such as "Dragutin's and Mira's son" or "Professor Volf"), I am now "Nathanael's father" (so that when I go to pick him up at his pre-school, a parent of another child might say to me, "Ah, so you are Nathanael's father!" and I would not be sure whether this is good or bad). I am not simply other than Nathanael; Nathanael is also part of who I am. My identity is inclusive, not exclusive. The same holds true of our other identities. To be a white American means to be in relation with black Americans, including the history of slavery and discrimination. It is no different with gender identity. What it means to be male will change over time and differ from place to place, but it will always be correlated with what it means to be female.[8] As Paul Ricoeur puts it in *Oneself as Another*, the "selfhood of oneself implies otherness to such an intimate degree that one cannot be thought of without the other, that instead one passes into the other."[9]

For such inclusive identity, two things are critically important, and they both concern boundaries. First, in order to have an identity, you must have boundaries. Imagine a world without boundaries. You cannot! For without boundaries you would not have "a world"; everything would be jumbled up together and nothing distinct would exist, which is to say that just about nothing would exist at all. To have anything except infinite chaos, you must have boundaries. Hence when God creates, God separates. If boundaries are good, then some kind of boundary maintenance must be good too. Hence when boundaries are threatened (as they often are in a variety of ways), they must be maintained. Second, if to have identity one must have boundaries, then to have inclusive identity one must have *permeable and flexible* boundaries. With impermeable and inflexible boundaries, a self or a group will ultimately remain alone, without the other. For the other to come in and change the self or a group, the other must be let in (and, likely after a while also politely let out!).

Our homes provide good examples of complex and dynamic identities circumscribed by permeable and flexible boundaries. When I go to a foreign land I like to buy a local work of art. I bring it home and place it in our living room, my office, or wherever. A space that is properly our own contains a number of "foreign" objects. They are windows into worlds that have become part of me—Cambridge, Madras, Prague, St. Petersburg, Zagreb. As such, they are also symbols of an identity that is not self-enclosed, but marked by *porous* boundaries and therefore shaped by the other. Occasionally, I move a work of art to a different room to make space for another. Sometimes it even ends up in the basement. Something analogous happens with our identity. We enter new relationships and they shape us; certain things recede into the background and others receive new importance. We live as ourselves in that things which make up our identity multiply, shift, and change. Our boundaries are *flexible* and our identity dynamic.

Some of that change simply happens to us. Others with whom we are in close contact change, and as a consequence we change too. Nathanael came into our family, and I changed, whether I wanted to change or not. Moreover, I changed in ways that I could not fully control. Relationships are by definition made up of more actors than one, and persons can react to the presence and action of others, but they can neither control fully that to which they will react nor the conditions under which they will react. Chance and unpredictability come with having permeable and flexible boundaries. At the same time, we can refuse movement of our identity in certain directions and we can initiate movements in other directions. In encounters with others we are not a rudderless boat at high seas. We can significantly craft our identity, and in the process we can even help shape the identities of others.

Who are we? We are people with inclusive and changing identities; multiple others are part of who we are. We can try to eject them from ourselves in order to craft for ourselves an exclusive identity, but we will then do violence not only to others, but also to ourselves. Who is the other? Earlier I have argued that others are our neighbors who differ from us by culture and whose very otherness is often a factor in our conflicts with them. Now, after the discussion of inclusive identity, we can say that the others are also not *just* others. They too have complex and dynamic identities, of which we are part, if we are their neighbors. Just as we are "inhabited" by others and have a history with them, others are also "inhabited" by us. If persons and groups are attuned to such complex and dynamic identities, they will not relate to each other according to simple binary schemata "I am I and you are you" (in case of persons) or "you are either in or out" (in case of groups). Their relations will be correspondingly complex. How do such complex relations look?

HOW SHOULD WE RELATE TO EACH OTHER?

I will analyze relations of persons with inclusive and dynamic identities under four headings: (1) The will to embrace the other; (2) Inverting perspectives; (3) Engagement with the other; and (4) Embracing the other. The four headings follow a certain order of priority, but they are not simply sequential so that when you complete one step you go to the next. Since they are significantly involved in each other, they are best done by foregrounding one or the other while simultaneously not disregarding the others.

THE WILL TO EMBRACE THE "OTHER"

In a sense, the commitment to live with others is the simplest aspect of our relation with them. Yet, it is often the most difficult one. Instead of considering others as my own diminishment, I have to imagine them as potential enrichment. Instead of thinking that they disfigure my social landscape, I have to think of them as potentially contributing to its aesthetic improvement. Instead of only suspecting enemies, I have to see them as potential friends.

We have reasons for wanting to keep others at bay. For one, we are afraid for our *identity*. Above all we fear being overwhelmed by others and their ways. There is a German word for this fear: *Überfremdung*. It is as if a guest in your home would start to bring in her own furniture and rearrange and take out yours, cook food and play music you do not like, and bang around working when you would like to sleep. So you say to your guest as politely as you can, "This is *my* home, and this is not how I want to live. Go back to your own place, and there you can live as you please. Here we are going to live as I please." Earlier I mentioned that globalization brings others into our proximity. The consequence is often the feeling of *Überfremdung*. Smaller cultures, like the Macedonian and the Albanian, are threatened by the huge wave of global mono-culture washing over them. They are attracted to many of its features, but they fear that the centuries-long, rich traditions which give them a sense of identity will be replaced by a culture foreign and shallow. Prosperous Western democracies worry that the processes of globalization, which bring to their lands people in search of better living, will undermine the very culture that made possible the freedoms and prosperity which they enjoy.

Second, we fear for our *safety*. The myth of an "innocent other" is just that—a myth. Relationships between people are always sites of contested power, and there is a permanent danger of misuse of power, especially between those who are reciprocally "other." Yet we should guard lest we, in refusing to accept the myth of the innocent other, embrace two other myths at the same time: the myth of the "innocent self" and of the "demonic other."

Third, *old enmities* make us hesitate about living with the other. We know that old wounds can lead to new injuries. History has a way of repeating itself. But, even when our safety is reasonably assured, either because we have become more powerful or because both parties have been inserted into a larger network of relations which guarantee our safety, we may still hesitate about living together with the other on moral grounds. Would positive relations with the other not amount to betrayal of our ancestors who have suffered at others' hands? Would we not betray ourselves if we reconciled with our former enemy? Finally, the brute fact of enmity pushes against the commitment to consociality. Just like sin in general according to the Christian tradition, enmity has power. Once established, it is a force beyond the individual wills of actors, and it perpetuates itself by holding enemies captive.

Our sense of identity, fear for safety, and old enmities all militate against the will to embrace the other. So why should we want to embrace the other? First, it may be in our *interest* to do so. The alternatives—either building a wall of separation or perpetuating enmity—are often much worse. As proximate others, we are intertwined by bonds of economy, culture, and family. Severing these bonds can be worse than trying to live together, as the example of the war in Bosnia shows. But the more important reason is that living with the other in peace is an expression of our God-given *humanity*. We are created not to isolate ourselves from others but to engage them, indeed, to contribute to their flourishing, as we nurture our own identity and attend to our own well-being. Finally, for Christians, the most important reason for being willing not only to live with others, but positively to embrace them is the character of God's love as displayed in Jesus Christ. Jesus Christ died for all human beings because he loved them all. Though not divine and though in no way capable of redeeming anyone, human beings, too, should love indiscriminately, each and every human being, including not only "the other" but also the enemy.[10]

We may be persuaded that it is good to embrace others, and we may want to embrace them, but still find ourselves unable to do so. Our fears and enmities may get the best of us. Our previous failures may make us lose hope. How do we acquire the will to embrace the other? How do we sustain it through difficult times? Let me try to answer these questions with a story. I was in Zagreb, Croatia, speaking at the promotion of the Croatian translation of my book *Exclusion and Embrace.* As I was explaining the idea of "will to embrace," which is central to the book's argument, I noticed a person in the audience who was listening intently but restlessly. After I finished my lecture and the crowd had cleared, he almost charged toward me and said, "But where does it come from?" And I said, "Where does what come from?" He said, "Where does the will to embrace come from?" He was agitated. He went on, "Is it inborn? Can one learn to will in such ways?" We went together through different possibilities. Ultimately, I said, the will to embrace comes from the divine Spirit of embrace, which can open up our self-enclosed sense of identity, dispel our fears, and break down the hold of enmity over us.

The appeal to the Spirit does not exclude other sources of the will to embrace but includes them. The Spirit of embrace is the Creator Spirit, who has fashioned human beings to live in loving relationships with others. So we may well be motivated by the fulfillment that love provides. The Spirit of embrace is also the Redeemer Spirit, who is calling us into being communities which embody and through their practices transmit the will to embrace. So our characters may be shaped through communities of embrace. And yet ultimately the source of the will is that same Spirit which rested on Jesus Christ and led Him to die for the ungodly.

INVERTING PERSPECTIVES

To live out the will to embrace we need to engage in inverting perspectives. But before we discuss "inverting perspectives," it is important to note one important feature of otherness. It is a reciprocal relation: if others are "other" to me, then I am an "other" to them. This is especially important to keep in mind in cases when otherness is not just a neutral term to describe difference, but when otherness acquires derogatory connotations, when to be other means not to be as good in some regard as I am myself.

Let me illustrate what I mean. When I was a doctoral student in Germany, along with many other Croats (as well as Greeks, Italians, Turks, and others) I felt like a second-class citizen. I was an *Ausländer,* and for many Germans

Ausländers are by definition deficient in some important ways. Once I was given a ride to Croatia by a porter of my dormitory who was driving there for a vacation. After we crossed the border I made a joking comment, "Now you are an *Ausländer!*" He did not think this was funny. In his mind, a German was a German and never an *Ausländer*. And yet that cannot be. If I am *Ausländer* in his home country, then he is *Ausländer* in mine; the relationship is reciprocal. The denial of reciprocity is in part what constitutes a prideful and injurious denigration of the other.

Once we understand the reciprocity involved in the relation of otherness, we will have more reasons to be interested not only in what we think about ourselves and about others, but also in what others think of themselves and of us. This is what I mean by "inverting perspectives." There are pragmatic reasons for this endeavor. As Rowan Williams has written in his comments on the terrorist attack on the World Trade Center entitled *Writing in the Dust*, "we have to see that we have a life in other people's imagination, quite beyond our control."[11] Not attending to other people's imaginations of us may be dangerous. But there are also moral reasons for this inverting of perspectives. Commitments to truth, to justice, to life in peace with others all require it. We cannot live truthful, just, and peaceful lives with others in a complex world if the only perspective we are willing to entertain is our own. To be unwilling to engage in inverting perspectives is to live, as Immanuel Kant put it, as a self-enclosed one-eyed Cyclops in need of another eye which would let him see things from the perspective of other people.

What does inverting perspectives entail? First, we need to *see others through their own eyes*. It is natural for us to see them with our own eyes, from our own perspective. To see others through their own eyes takes a willingness to entertain the possibility that we may be wrong and others right in their assessment of themselves, a leap of imagination to place ourselves in their position, a temporary bracketing of our own understanding of them, and receptive attention to their own story about who they see themselves to be.

Second, we need to *see ourselves through the eyes of others*. Sometimes we think that if we know anything well, it is ourselves that we know well. But I can fail to see something well not simply because it is too distant, but also because it is too close. Moreover, when it comes to myself, I have a vested interest in seeing myself in a certain way—noticing that what is positive but not what is negative, or letting that which is positive overshadow or relativize the negative. Because we often fail to see ourselves adequately, we need to learn how we are perceived by others. Take as an example the debate on so-called Orientalism (the stereotypes that the Christian West has about the Muslim East) and Occidentalism (the stereotypes that the Muslim East has about the Christian West). Where the West may see itself as "prosperous," the East may see it as "decadent"; where the West may see itself as "freedom loving," the East may see it as "oppressive"; where the West may see itself as "rational," the East may see it as "calculating."[12] It is important for the West to see itself from the perspective of the East, and to inquire seriously as to the adequacy of its own self-perception in light of the way it is perceived. The same, of course, holds true for the East.

Inverting perspectives is second nature for the weak. In encounters with the strong, they always have to attend to how they and their actions are perceived by the strong. Their success and even survival depend on seeing themselves with the eyes of the other. The strong are not in the habit of taking into account what the weak think of them; they can do without inverting perspective. If the weak do not like what they see, so much the worse for the weak. If the only thing that matters to the strong is power and privilege, they will charge ahead, without regard for the perspective of the weak. But if they want to be truthful and just, they will want the weak to free them from their own false judgments of themselves and of their relations with others.

ENGAGEMENT WITH THE "OTHER"

To see oneself and the other from the perspective of the other is not the same as agreeing with the other. *As* I invert perspective, I bracket my own self-understanding and the understanding of the other, and I suspend judgment. *After* I have understood how the other wishes to be understood and how the other understands me, I must exercise judgment and either agree or disagree, wholly or in part. This is where argumentative engagement comes in.

I could refuse to engage the other with arguments. I could simply insist that I am right. But the result would be irreconcilable clashing of perspectives. In the absence of arguments, the relative power of social actors would decide the outcome. True, we cannot argue interminably, for life would then have to stop. As we are in fact acting even when we are waiting to resolve our own intellectual questions—there is no exit from acting, as William James has argued in "The Will to Believe"[13]—so we will be acting even as we are waiting to argue through our differences in perspectives. But we can act in our best light, and then return to argument. In fact, this is what citizens in well-functioning democracies do: they argue, they vote, and then, if some of them do not like the result, they argue and vote again. And as Nicholas Wolterstorff has suggested, they do so even when a larger polity does not have "a shared political basis," but lives with "a politics of multiple communities."[14]

Some would argue that arguments cannot be rationally adjudicated across multiple communities. There is no common ground between them, the argument goes, and therefore we are left with conflicting rationalities, which is to say that we are left with conflict.[15] But the claim that there is no common ground between "others" seems patently false. Commenting on a picture of people marching in the streets of Prague with signs which simply say "Truth" and "Justice," Michael Walzer writes, "When I saw the picture, I knew immediately what the signs meant—and so did everyone else who saw the same picture. Not only that: I also recognized and acknowledged the values that the marchers were defending—and so did (almost) everyone else."[16] Even if we all have our own maximalist definitions of moral terms shaped by culturally specific and "thick" morality, we also share minimalist moral definitions which "are embedded in the maximal morality."[17] We can argue successfully over cultural boundary lines because we understand and for the most part acknowledge minimalist definitions of relevant terms. When incommensurability threatens between diverse communities, it is not because in principle rational argumentation between them is impossible, but because the readiness to seek through common discourse the truth which transcends one's own convictions is lacking, or because the communities do not possess even an elementary willingness to share the same social space.

Positive engagement with the other is not just a matter of argument. Even when arguments fail to bring anything like consensus or convergence, we can still cooperate in many ways, unless a dispute concerns acts of grave injustice. The belief that we must agree on overarching interpretative frameworks and all essential values in order to live in peace is mistaken. It ultimately presupposes that peace can exist only if cultural sameness reigns. But even if one considered such sameness desirable, it is clearly unachievable. Take major world religions as an example. A consensus between them on overarching interpretations of the world is not on the horizon in the near future. Must their adherents be therefore at war with one another? Of course not—they can live in peace and cooperate, their fundamental disagreements notwithstanding, and they can do so out of their own properly religious resources. Though the practice of Christians sometimes seems to falsify this claim, everything in the Christian faith itself speaks in favor of it, from the simple and explicit injunction to live in peace with *all* people (Rom. 12:18) to the character of God as triune love.[18]

EMBRACE OF THE "OTHER"

A simple willingness to embrace the other does not suffice. A further step of actually embracing them is needed. As we are arguing with others about issues of truth and justice, we are making sure that embrace, if it takes place, will not be a sham, a denial of truth and a trampling on justice. As we are engaged in inverting perspectives, we have started embracing others in that we have taken them, even if only in a symbolic form and for a time, into our own selves; we have made their eyes our own. But for embrace to take place, more is needed. We need to make space for them in our own identity and in our social world (though how that space will be made remains open for negotiations). We need to let them reshape our identity so as to become part of who we are, yet without in any way threatening or obliterating us but rather helping to establish the rich texture of our identity. Just as after the birth of my second son, Aaron, I let him be inserted, so to speak, into my identity, so also we ought to let our proximate others be a part of who we are (adjusted, of course, for the differences between family and neighbor relations). To use a local example, this would mean that Albanians living in Macedonia would not see themselves as just Albanians; they would see themselves as Albanians, whose identity consists in part in being neighbors to Macedonians and sharing a larger Macedonian political space with them. The same, adjusted to account for the differences between the two groups, holds true for Macedonians.

Such welcome is possible on Christian terms because we Christians should not think of ourselves as having a pure national, cultural, racial, or ethnic identity. Not only do we, along with Jews and Muslims, believe that all human beings are creatures of one God, we also believe that the humanity which unites humans is more significant than any difference that may divide them. Further, an image of the Christian life which looms large in the Bible and in the Christian tradition is that of a *pilgrim*. A pilgrim is not defined primarily by the land or culture through which he or she is traveling, but by the place toward which he or she is on the way; his or her primary identity comes from the destination, not from any point along the journey. And the land toward which Christians are moving is God's new world, in which people from "all tribes and languages" will be gathered. Being a pilgrim does not exclude a whole range of secondary identities, such as a citizen of Macedonia, ethnic Romany, woman, and mother of three rebellious teenagers. But in Christian understanding, all these identities ought to be subordinated to the primary identity as a person on the way to God's new world.

The unsettling of Christians' sense of cultural identity cuts deep. The Apostle Paul writes that Christians "are not their own." This is a strange thing to say. A lot of things are my own, and I guard them carefully. And it would seem that what is more my own than anything else is myself. And yet the Apostle insists that we are not our own, but belong to the Lord. As a Christian in Paul's sense, I am so much not myself that "it is no longer I who live, but it is Christ who lives in me" (Gal. 2:20). Christian identity is taken out of our own hands and placed into the hands of the divine Other, and by this it is both radically unsettled and unassailably secured. Because Christ defines *our* identity in the primary way, Christians can confidently set on a journey with proximate others and engage without fear in the give-and-take of the relationship with others that marks an inclusive identity. What will be the result of this engagement? Like Abraham's, it will be a journey of faith and hope toward the land which one has not yet seen.

But should we not maintain our boundaries so as to protect our cultural identities? Yes, we should. If I am crushed in the process of embrace with the other, this is no longer an embrace but an act of covert aggression. Whereas the *will* to embrace the other is unconditional, the *embrace itself* is not. It is conditioned, first, on the preservation of the integrity of the self. Boundaries are good, I argued earlier, because discrete identities themselves are a good. And because both are good, they have to be protected. Earlier I have argued for protection of identities—of one's self and of one's group—by appealing to *creation*. To have anything distinct at all and therefore to have "a world," you must have and maintain boundaries. Hence when God creates, God separates (and binds together, of course). One can argue for protection of identities also on the basis of *redemption*. Since God showed redeeming love in Christ for all humanity, the self cannot be excluded as a legitimate object of love. I should love myself, provided my love of self is properly related to the love of God and of the neighbor.[19] And since I can love myself, I can certainly love my group because such love includes both the love of the neighbor and the love of the self (since my own well-being is often connected with the well-being of my group). Hence one is entitled to ensure that the embrace of the other does not endanger the self.

Moreover, the embrace is predicated on the settling of the disputes with the other around the questions of truth and justice. How should these questions be settled? For Christians, the guardian at the boundaries of identity is Christ, and the self inhabited by Christ is therefore committed to making the story of Jesus Christ his or her own story. A one-word summary of that story is *grace*. Now grace is grace only against the backdrop of the law of justice. I am gracious in situations of conflict if I forego the rightful claims of the law, forgive, and reconcile with the other. I am gracious in situations of need if I do not only what the law of justice prescribes, but also engage in acts of generosity toward the needy. In the act of grace, the law of justice is not inoperative; to the contrary, its demands are implicitly recognized as valid. In showing grace, however, I "transgress" the law of justice, not by doing less than it requires, but by doing more.[20] Two things follow from this understanding of grace. First, grace is very much compatible with ongoing arguments between parties about what relations between them would be just and with the demand that one not be treated unjustly. Second, the receiver of grace has no claim on the grace of the giver; though the giver may be obliged to give (as Christians are obliged to forgive), the receiver cannot demand to be given.

The four elements of relating to the other— commitment to consociality, inverting perspectives, engagement, and embrace—leave many thorny issues unresolved. I have said nothing about political arrangements most suitable for living with multiple others. Nicholas Wolterstorff has argued for a particular kind of liberal democracy as best suited for culturally and religiously pluralistic societies. It has two features that distinguish it from other conceptions of liberal democracy, notably from that of John Rawls. First, it is not necessary to have a shared political basis rooted in the idea of public reason. Instead, we should learn to live "with the politics of multiple communities."[21] Second, the state should be "neutral with respect to the religious and other comprehensive perspectives present in society," and that neutrality should be understood "as requiring *impartiality* of the state with respect to all comprehensive perspectives rather than *separation* of the state from all of them.[22] I share Wolterstorff's position. Important as the four elements of relating to the other that I have analyzed are in their own right, they can be also seen as part of an *ethos* of a genuinely pluralistic liberal democracy of the kind Wolterstorff advocates.

"THE BROTHER" AND THE "OTHER"

Let me conclude by making one qualification. The last part of my paper— *How Should We Relate to Each Other?*—is predicated on an important but contested persuasion. It is that we should relate to the other not simply as a bearer of rights, but also as a proper object of love.

In *The Ethics of Memory* Avishai Margalit has distinguished what he calls "the Christian project" from "the Jewish project." The Christian project, he writes, "is an effort to establish, in historical time, an ethical community based on love. This community, ideally, should include all of humanity, and it should be based on the memory of the cross as an ultimate sacrifice for the sake of humanity."[23] In contrast, the Jewish project

> retains the double tier of ethics and morality at least for historical times, and postpones the idea of a universal ethical community to the messianic era. Jews are obliged to establish themselves as an ethical community of caring. The force of the obligation is gratitude to God for having delivered their ancestors from the 'house of slaves' in Egypt. . . . In distinction from ethics, morality, in the Jewish view, is based on a different source. It is based on the debt of gratitude all humanity owes God for having been created in His image.[24]

The basic obligation in the first-tier communal ethics is care, and the basic obligation in the second-tier universal morality is respect. To the brother—whether he is a family member, compatriot, or co-religionist—we owe care; to the other, we owe respect.

In Margalit's terms, I was engaged in this paper in "the Christian project." I have not reserved love for "the brother," but applied it to "the other" as well. As he rightly notes, for Christians love applies to the other because the central saving event, the death and resurrection of Jesus Christ, concerns *every* human being. As God loved "the world" and "gave his only Son" (Jn. 3:16), so Christians are obliged to love every human being. But noble as it may be to consider the whole human commonwealth as an ethical community of love, is it not also an impossible ideal? So it is. Theologians have rarely advocated that it takes, as Margalit puts it, only "a little helping of grace" for humanity to "be established as an ethical community of love."[25] Much like Jews, Christians have left the realization of this ideal to God's intervention at the end of the age. But still they have refused to correlate "love" with "thick" relations and "respect" with "thin" relations. Love and respect apply to both kinds of relations.

But do not people to whom we are "thickly" related demand special attention? A spouse and children seem to do so. Why not fellow members of the same ethnic group? Insisting that "every human being is my neighbor," some Christians have advocated that we should be impartial in our love, extending it to those to whom we are "thinly" related no less than to those to whom we are "thickly" related. Yet even those Christian theologians who, like Augustine in *Teaching Christianity*, claim that "all people should be loved equally,"[26] insist that "proximity" makes a difference. Augustine writes, "since you cannot be of service to everyone, you have to take greater care of those who are more closely joined to you by a turn, so to say, of fortune's wheel, whether by occasion of place or time, or any other such circumstance."[27] Other Christian theologians, like Thomas Aquinas in *Summa Theologica*, have claimed that all neighbors should not be loved equally; we have special relations to some people and "the union arising from natural origin is prior to, and more stable than, all others."[28] So to claim that love's scope is universal does not imply that we do not differentiate in how we ought to love those with whom we have special relations and those with whom we do not.

There is no good reason to wed the claim that love is universal in scope with what Gene Outka has called "simplified egalitarianism" which does not take into account that "our capacity for reciprocal help and harm is deeper and more varied with those closely related to us."[29] The Christian claim that we should "love" all people, not just those with whom we have special relations, does not imply undifferentiated cosmopolitanism, which would preclude giving special attention to our own family, ethnic group, nation, or broader culture. Not only is it right to maintain boundaries of discrete group identities, as I have argued earlier, it is also right to devote one's energies so that the group to which we belong will flourish. What Christians ought not to do, is fail to love "the other," especially the proximate other. This I take to be one of the points of the story of the Good Samaritan.

NOTES

1. A slightly edited version of "Living With the 'Other'," was published in a special double issue of *Journal of Ecumenical Studies*, Winter-Spring 2002, vol. 39:1–2; entitled *Interreligious Dialogue: Toward Reconciliation in Macedonia and Bosnia*. Edited by Paul Mojzes, Leonard Swidler, and Heinz-Gerhard Justenhoven. (Philadelphia: Ecumenical Press, 2003), p. 8–25. Used by permission.

2. John Hick, *An Interpretation of Religion: Human Responses to the Transcendent* (New Haven: Yale University Press, 1989), p. 233.

3. Michael Barnes, *Theology and the Dialogue of Religions* (Cambridge: Cambridge UP, 2002), p. 182.

4. See, for instance, Michael Theunissen, *Der Andere. Studien zur Sozialontologie der Gegenwart* (Berlin: Walter de Gruyter, 1977); Tzvetan Todorov, *The Conquest of America: The Question of the Other*, transl. Richard Howard (New York: HarperCollins, 1984); Enrique Dussel, *The Invention of the Americas: Eclipse of 'the Other' and the Myth of Modernity*, transl. M. D. Barber (New York: Continuum, 1985).

5. See Diana L. Eck, *A New Religious America: How A 'Christian Country' Has Become the World's Most Religiously Diverse Nation* (San Francisco: HarperCollins, 2001).

6. Primo Levi, *Survival in Auschwitz: The Nazi Assault on Humanity*, transl. Stuart Woolf (New York: Simon & Schuster, 1996), p. 9.

7. See Paul Ricoeur, *Oneself as Another*, transl. Kathleen Blamey (Chicago: The University of Chicago Press, 1992), pp. 2–4.

8. For this notion of gender identity see Miroslav Volf, *Exclusion and Embrace: A Theological Exploration of Identity, Otherness, and Reconciliation* (Nashville: Abingdon Press, 1996), pp. 174–176.

9. Ricoeur, p. 3.

10. In the Christian tradition, the universal scope of love was historically grounded in the common Adamic descent of all human beings and in Christ's death on the cross for all human beings (see Gene Outka, "Universal Love and Impartiality," *The Love Commandments: Essays in Christian Ethics and Moral Philosophy*, eds. Edmund N. Santurri and William Werpehowski (Washington, D.C.: Georgetown University Press, 1992), p. 9).

11. Rowan Williams, *Writing in the Dust: After September 11* (Grand Rapids: Eerdmans, 2002), p. 55.

12. See Avishai Margalit and Ian Buruma, "Occidentalism," *New York Review of Books* (January 2002). Online at http://www.nybooks.com/articles/15100.

13. William James, "The Will to Believe," *The Will to Believe and Other Essays in Popular Philosophy and Human Immortality* (New York: Dover Publications, 1956), pp. 1–31.

14. Nicholas Wolterstorff, "The Role of Religion in Decision and Discussion of Political Issues," in Robert Audi and Nicholas Wolterstorff, *Religion in the Public Square: The Place of Religious Convictions in Political Debate* (Lanham: Rowman & Littlefield Publishers, 1997), p. 109.

15. See, for instance, Stanley Fish, "Why We Can't All Just Get Along," *First Things*, 60 (2/1996), pp. 18–26.

16. Michael Walzer, *Thick and Thin: Moral Argument at Home and Abroad* (Notre Dame: University of Notre Dame Press, 1994), p. 1.

17. Walzer, p. 3.

18. See Miroslav Volf, "Christianity and Violence," (forthcoming).

19. For an argument that the self is a proper object of love see Outka, "Universal Love and Impartiality," pp. 1–103.

20. Hence the possibility to interpret "mercy" as injustice (see Jeffrie Murphy, "Mercy and Legal Justice," Jeffrie G. Murphy and Jean Hampton, *Forgiveness and Mercy* (Cambridge: Cambridge University Press, 1988), p. 169.

21. Nicholas Wolterstorff, "The Role of Religion," p. 109.

22. Wolterstorff, p. 115.

23. Margalit, *The Ethics of Memory*, p. 71.

24. Margalit, p. 72.

25. Ibid., p. 72.

26. Augustine, *Teaching Christianity*, transl. Edmund Hill, in *The Works of Saint Augustine: A Translation for the 21st Century I/11* (Hyde Park: New City Press, 1996), I, p. 29.

27. Ibid

28. Thomas Aquinas, *Summa Theologica*, transl. Fathers of the English Dominican Province (Westminster: Christian Classics, 1981), IIa IIae, q.26, a8.

29. Outka, "Universal Love and Impartiality," p. 91.

Chapter Two

TOWARD COMMON GROUND IN UNDERSTANDING THE HUMAN CONDITION

J. Dudley Woodberry
Professor of Islamic Studies
Fuller Theological Seminary

Traditionally Christians and Muslims have understood their Scriptures to give very different diagnoses of the human condition and consequently have understood the solutions to be very different. In this paper we shall look first at the reasons for this understanding. Then, by noting some additional references, we shall suggest that there is more common ground than is normally observed, and suggest that consequently there can be more agreement on the type of solution required.

TRADITIONAL CONTRASTING UNDERSTANDINGS

We shall look briefly at the biblical and qur'anic narratives of Adam and Eve, how they start similarly and then begin to diverge. Then we shall see how their implications diverge further in subsequent writings in the Christian and Islamic traditions.

Scriptural Narratives

The Bible in the Torah identifies two characteristics in humans, Adam (the name means "humankind") was created in God's image (Genesis 1:26–27) but disobeyed God for which he was banished from the Garden (Genesis 3). The Qur'an does not say that Adam was created in the image of God but does state that humankind's original state (*fitra*) was that of a pristine monotheist (*hanif*) and "there is no alteration of the creation of God" (al-Rum [30]:30). As in the Torah Adam disobeyed God (Ta-Ha [20]:121), was banished from the Garden (al-Baqara [2]:36–37), but unlike the biblical account he "forgot" and did not "intend" to sin (Ta-Ha [20]:115).

Authoritative Witnesses

The Gospel (*Injil*) goes on to say that following the pattern of Adam all humans sin (Romans 5:12). The Apostle Paul describes his own condition as that of the human race: he wants to do good but is a slave to the inclination to sin (Romans 7:14–24). The Canonical Hadith echo the Bible when al-Bukhari reports the prophetic tradition that God created Adam in His image (*suratihi*).[1] They also reiterate the creation of humans in a pristine state (*fitra*) but then add that their parents make them Jewish, Christian, or Magian.[2]

Subsequent Interpreters

Christian writers have tended like Cyril of Alexandria to note that humanity's fallen condition is both natural because we all incline toward sin and contrary to nature because we are made in the image of God even though it is distorted by sin.[3] Muslim writers like Badru Kateregga have normally maintained that "man is fundamentally a good and dignified creature. He is not a fallen being."[4] Thus there is similarity between Christian and Muslim understandings of the purity of Adam's original state, but a difference in traditional understandings of humanity today. Whereas the Qur'an says that "there is no alteration in the creation of God" (al-Rum [30]:30), Christians have noted humanity's fallenness while still retaining the image of God in marred form.

TOWARD COMMON GROUND

When we look more closely at the sources identified in the previous section, I suggest that we can find more common ground than often noted.

Scriptural Narratives

The Bible by using the name Adam (which means "humankind") indicates that he represents humans in general, as we have noted. Also, we have observed that he was made in the image of God though it was marred by sin.

Therefore, in any comparison with Islamic sources and human experience in general, we need to look for both the good and the bad tendencies in humans. The Qur'an in the *fitra* concept includes the good tendencies of humans. A closer look at the Adam and Eve narrative, however, shows more parallels with the biblical account of the "fall" than are normally noted.

First, there is an awareness that, if humans are created, then they will be corrupt. With reference to the creation of Adam we read:

> And when the Lord said to the angels, "I am setting in the earth a viceroy," they said, "What, will You set therein one who will do corruption there, and shed blood, while we proclaim Your praise and call You holy?" He said, "Assuredly I know what you know not" (al-Baqara [2]:30/28).

The subsequent qur'anic account confirms that corruption and sin against other humans is what resulted when they were given power and freedom. God's response indicates a knowledge of this and, it would appear, a solution.

Secondly, the Devil (*Iblis*) foretells that he will master and pervert most people. After he disobeyed God, by refusing to bow down to Adam, he says, "I shall assuredly subjugate his seed, save a few" (al-Isra' [17]:62/64). In another account of the story, Satan tells God, "As You have perverted me, I will sit in ambush for them. . . . You will not find most of them grateful" (al-A'raf [7]:16/15-17/16). In still another rendering of the story Iblis says, "As You have perverted me . . . I shall pervert them, all together, except those of Your servants among them that are devoted" (al-Hijr [15]:39–40). Subsequent history in the Qur'an and human experience have shown these not to be idle boasts. They have been difficult facts to explain if humans are basically good.

Thirdly, some verses reflect the biblical perspective that Adam knowingly disobeyed or rebelled against the will of God. The account of the fall of Adam in Sura Ta-Ha [20] starts with the biblical concept of a covenant: "We [God] made a covenant (*'ahidna*) with Adam before" (Ta-Ha [20]:115). As we have noted, Muslims have tended to focus on Adam's subsequent forgetfulness in the same verse, but this is hard to correlate with Satan's reminder to Adam and Eve of God's prohibition (al-A'raf [7]:20/19). In fact, the subsequent eating of the fruit is described in very strong words: "Adam rebelled against (or disobeyed—*'asa*) his Lord and went astray (or erred—*faghawa*)" (Ta-Ha [20]:121/119). This latter description reiterates the biblical portrayal of his sin as disobedience and rebellion.

When we probe deeper to ascertain the nature of the rebellion, we note, fourthly, that in both the Bible and the Qur'an, Adam rejects the type of creaturehood that God has assigned to him even though the details are different. In the Bible the temptation is to become "like God knowing good and, evil, "and they ate of the Tree of the Knowledge of Good and Evil (Gen. 2:17;

3:5–6). In the Qur'an the temptation is to "become angels or . . . immortals" (al-A'raf [7]:20/19), and they ate of the Tree of Immortality (Ta-Ha [20]:120/118-121/119), which was barred to them by the cherubim in the Genesis account (3:24). In both renderings, however, Adam and Eve reject their form of creaturehood assigned by the Creator.

Fifthly, with respect to who was responsible for Adam and Eve's disobedience, they said, "Lord, we have wronged ourselves" (al-A'raf [7]:23/22), indicating they were at fault.[5] When we look, sixthly, at the results of their action, we again note biblical parallels. They have a sense of shame (al-A'raf [7]:22/21; 20:121/119). While the Qur'an implies they consequently hide from God, the eminent historian and commentator al-Tabari (224–241 A.H./839–855 A.D.) quotes Wahb ibn Munabbih as making this explicit: Adam hides in a tree because "I feel ashamed before You, O Lord."[6] They confess that unless God forgives them and has mercy on them they will be "among the lost" (al-A'raf [7]:23/22). They are expelled from Paradise and have enmity between them (al-Baqara [2]:36/34, 38/36; al-A'raf [7]:24/23, Ta-Ha [20]:123/121).

The question arises as to whether or not the Qur'an indicates any implications of these events for the human race. As for the expulsion from Paradise, al-Baqara [2]:38/36 puts the command in the Arabic plural form, indicating more than two ("Get you down out of it, all together"), rather than in the dual form ("Get you down, both of you together" (Ta-Ha [20]:123/121). Muslim commentators have normally accounted for this plural by including Iblis in the expulsion with Adam and Eve.[7] The same verses declare enmity between those expelled. Does the story of "the fall" give any insight into our nature? Surah al-A'raf [7]:26/25-27/26 makes it an illustration and warning about Satan's continued temptations to the "Children of Adam."

Satan's prediction that he would master and pervert most humans (al-A'raf [7]:16/15-16/17; al-Hijr [15]:39–40; al-Isra' [17]:62/64) is borne out in the subsequent qur'anic narrative.[8] After Adam and Eve disobeyed, the Children of Adam are warned, "Let not Satan tempt you as he brought your parents out of the Garden" (al-A'raf [7]:27/26). Next Cain murders Abel (al-Ma'ida [5]:27/30-30/33). Each community is sent an Apostle (al-Nahl [16]:36/38), but one after another they reject him—the people of Noah, the companions of the Rass, and Thamud, and Ad, and Pharaoh, the brothers of Lot, the men of the Grove (Midian), and the people of Tubba' (Qaf [50]:12-14/13). Others are added—the people of Abraham and Moses and many cities (al-Hajj [22]:42/93-45/44). Generation after generation were destroyed when they did evil (Yunus [10]:13/14; al-Isra' [17]:17/18; Maryam [19]:98, etc.).

There were exceptions such as those to whom Jonah preached (10:98), but the majority seem to be evil:

We sent Noah and Abraham, and We appointed the Prophecy and the Book to be among their seed; and some of them go aright while many of them are perverse (al-Hadid [57]:26).

If only there had been among the generations before you men of perseverance restraining from corruption in the earth—except a few of these whom We delivered from amongst them (Hud [11]:116/118).

The portrayal goes on: "Most men are not believers" (Yusuf [12]:103); "Most of them do not believe in God" (Yusuf [12]:106); "Most men do not believe" (al-Ra'd [13]:1). The Qur'an recounts, "We sent Apostles among the people of old, and not a single Apostle came without them mocking him" (al-Hijr [15]:10–11). Again the question arises: If people are basically good, how do we account for the qur'anic witness that most people rejecting right guidance?

We have noted Sura al-Rum [30]:30, the verse traditionally used to indicate the state of natural purity (*fitra*) in which people are created. There are, however, many other verses which indicate a more critical human predicament. Perhaps the clearest of these is Sura Yusuf [12]:53, where Joseph refers to his temptation with Potiphar's wife and says, "The soul is certainly an inciter to evil." This does not place the blame on Satan or Potiphar's wife, but indicates a problem at the core of human nature. This statement carries added force because it comes from Joseph, as the text indicates and most commentators concur, rather than from Potiphar's wife.

Other passages refer to humankind as sinful (or unjust—*zulum*; Ibrahim [14]:34/37; al-Ahzab [33]:72), foolish (al-Ahzab [33]:72), ungrateful (Ibrahim [14]:34/37), weak (al-Nisa [4]:28/32), despairing or boastful (Hud [11]:9/12-10/13), quarrelsome (al-Nahl [16]:4), and rebellious (al-'Alaq [96]:6). The Qur'an concludes, "If God were to punish men for their wrongdoing (or injustice—*zulm*), he would not leave on earth a single creature" (al-Nahl [16]:61/63). If this is the verdict, is there not a need for a radical solution?

Authoritative Witnesses

The Gospel does not teach, as some believe, that Adam's guilt is passed on to the whole race. Romans 5:12 rather says, "death spread to all because all have sinned." Here we see the shared inheritance of sin and its influence on the one hand and individual responsibility on the other.

The Traditions, commentaries, and histories bring out more common ground with the biblical material. The canonical traditionist Muslim (202–261 A.H./817–875 A.D.), however, makes a connection between the sin of Adam and the descent of the human race when he recounts a story by the

Prophet in which Moses says to Adam: "because of your sin you caused mankind to come down to earth."[9]

We have noted that the Qur'an declares enmity between those who were expelled from Paradise. Of particular interest is a comment on the enmity by al-Tabari, on the authority of Wahb ibn Munabbih, in which God says to the serpent, "You shall be an enemy to the children of Adam and you shall bite his heel, but wherever he finds you he shall crush your head."[10] This not only relates the events to subsequent generations of people but is an obvious reference to Genesis 3:15, which Christians have traditionally understood to refer to the conflict culminating in the crucifixion where Jesus is wounded by Satan but where the former ultimately defeats the latter.

Does the story of "the fall" give any insight into our nature? As we have seen, Sura al-A'raf [7]:26/25-27/26 makes it an illustration and warning about Satan's continued temptations to the "Children of Adam." The canonical traditionist Tirmidhi (d. ca. 270 A.H./883 A.D.) relates that the Prophet noted that Adam's descendants repeated the sin of their ancestor: "Adam forgot and ate of the tree and his offspring forgot; and Adam sinned and his offspring sinned."[11]

The Prophet associates a deficiency in humans to Adam and Eve, according to Ibn Sa'd (ca. 168 A.H./784 A.D.-230/845) in his biographical dictionary. Here the Arabian Prophet says, "As regards Adam and Eve men are like a deficient grain measure which they will never succeed in filling."[12] Since the next sentence is about the Judgment Day, the human deficiency is apparently a moral one.

The most celebrated traditionist al-Bukhari attributed to the Prophet the words, "Satan touches every child when it is born, whereupon it starts crying loudly, except Mary and her son."[13] This idea of something that needs to be corrected from the earliest stage of development is found even in Muhammad himself according to his earliest biographer, who quotes him as saying:

> Two men in white raiment . . . opened up my belly, extracted my heart and split it; then they extracted a black drop from it and threw it away; then they washed my heart and my belly with snow until they had thoroughly cleaned them.[14]

What is wrong becomes more specific in a tradition of Ibn Hanbal (164–241 A.H./780–855 A.D.), who lent his name to one of the orthodox schools of law. He relates that the companions of Muhammad confessed to him that "we have no control over our hearts." He did not take issue with their awareness of their condition but directed them to the qur'anic statement "God charges no soul save to its capacity" (al-Baqara [2]:286).[15]

Subsequent Interpreters

Christian writers have noted how a biblical perspective on sin helps to explain the polarities of human experience. Henri Blocher has pointed out that the complementary concepts of the image of God and the fall of humans help to explain such seemingly incompatible phenomena of human experience as the evil even in good people and the good in evil people, the shared inheritance of sin and individual decision, and the universal compulsion toward sin and individual responsibility.[16]

Muslim writers reflect some of these views. Kamil Husain does not go so far as to say that human nature has a bias to wrong, but he sees the story of Adam as symbolic of the human condition and as dealing with the fundamental nature of humans.[17] When the account is interpreted in this way, there can be much common ground for Muslims and Christians.

Another contemporary scholar from al-Azhar and Morocco, Uthman Yahya, goes further in recognizing a "fall" in the race. Unlike most Muslims, he distinguishes between humans in two distinct states:

> the first is his original constitution, the prototype created in the image of God, the second man in his actual condition. As contrasted with his prototype man in his actual state is feeble (al-Nisa [4]:28), despairing (al-Hud [11]:9), unjust (al-Ibrahim [14]:34), quarrelsome (al-Nahl [16]: 4), tyrannical (al-Alaq [96]:6), lost (al-Fil [105]:2) . . . . We see clearly in the light of these quotations that there are two distinct states of man: that of his original nature and that of his fall. But if with the sin of Adam man has lost the state of Eden, it is by the crime of Cain that this sin has entered actively into humanity. . . . if . . . man, as he actually is, is incapable of living in perfect blessedness, where is salvation and by what means is it to be made real?[18]

Yahya gives the traditional Muslim answer: divine guidance. Christians would ask, "Is this enough?"

When we move on into the development of Muslim theology and philosophy, we see the theme of *al-nafs al-ammara* (the uncontrolled appetitive soul or carnal desire) running throughout its literature.[19] It is always there to lead astray. Ibn Hazm (384–456 A.H./994–1064 A.D.), a champion of fundamentalist doctrine, believed that the human soul, if left to itself, spontaneously inclines to dishonesty.[20] What could be closer to a Pauline view of human nature?

The most celebrated of all Muslim theologians al-Ghazali (450–505 A.H./1058–1111 A.D.) believed that the fall is repeated for each individual. He identified in humans four kinds of base inclinations: those of savage animals, those of the beast, those inspired by the devil, and those arising from pride and ambition.[21] The Christian would certainly agree that each individual repeats the sin of Adam and would see the act as arising from pride and ambition as we rebel against our creaturehood and the obedience due our Creator.

Turning to contemporary Shi'ite thinkers, we see a clear awareness of evil in human nature. The internationally recognized scholar Sayyed Hossein Nasr, while believing there is a way of escape, speaks of the "limited prison" of a person's "carnal soul."[22] In an address delivered on the occasion of the inauguration of the president of Iran on September 4, 1985, it was stated that "man's calamity is his carnal desires, and this exists in everybody, and it is rooted in the nature of man."[23]

Since so much common ground is found between Christian and Muslim diagnoses of the human condition, the Christian asks if this does not call for more common ground in the solutions. Currently both faiths share the need for repentance and forgiveness and the importance of God's law to show us how to please God, but the Christian feels that the enormity of the problem calls for what the Prophet Jesus called the new birth (John 3:5) and the Apostle Paul calls the Spirit of life (Romans 8:2–11).

NOTES

1. *Sahih al-Bukhari: Arabic-English*, trans. Muhammad Muhsin Khan (Beirut: Dar Al Arabia, 1985), VIII, 160) (Bk. 74, chap. 1, trad. 246).

2. Bukhari, VI, 284 (Bk. 60, chap. 230, trad. 298).

3. Henri Blocher, *Original Sin: Illuminating the Riddle* (Grand Rapids, MI.: William B. Eerdmans Publ. Co., 1997), p.30 and n.

4. Badru D. Kateregga and David Shenk, *Islam and Christianity* (Nairobi: Uzima Press Ltd., 1980), p.109.

5. For interpretations of the meaning of the common qur'anic reflexive verb "to wrong oneself," see Muhammad Kamil Husain, "The Meaning of Zulm in the Qur'an," trans. and ed. Kenneth Cragg, *Muslim World*, XLIX (1959): pp. 196–212.

6. Abu Ja'far al-Tabari, *The Commentary on the Qur'an (Jami'al-Bayan 'an Ta'wil ay al-Qur'an)*, trans. and ed. J. Cooper (Oxford: Oxford University Press, 1987), p. 251.

7. Al-Tabari, *Jami'al-Bayan* (Cairo: Dar al-Ma'arif, 1332/1954), I, 535–36 in Mahmoud Ayoub, *The Qur'an and Its Interpreters*, I (Albany: State University of New York Press, 1984), p. 84.

8. Of help in preparing this section has been an unpublished paper by Ernest Hahn, "The Response of Nations to Their Prophets" (Toronto: Fellowship of Faith for Muslims, 1982).

9. *Mishkat al-Masabih*, trans. and ed. James Robson (Lahore: Sh. Muhammad Ashraf, 1963), I, p. 23 (Bk. 2, chap. 4, sec. 1).

10. *Jami'al-Bayan* (Cairo, 1954 ed.), I, pp. 524–26 in Ayoub, p. 83.

11. *Mishkat*, I, 31 (Bk. 1, chap. 4, sec. 3).

12. *Kitab al-Tabaqat al-Kabir*, I (Leiden, 1905), 11–16 in *A Reader on Islam*, ed. Arthur Jeffery ('s-Gravenhage: Mouton & Co., 1962), p. 190.

13. *Sahih al-Bukhari*, VI, p. 54 (Bk. 60, chap. 54, trad. 71).

14. Ibn Hisham, ed., *The Life of Muhammad*: [Ibn] Ishaq's Sirat Rasul Allah, trans. A. Guillaume (London: Oxford University Press, 1955), p. 72.

15. Ibn Hanbal, no. 3071 in Kenneth Cragg and Marston Speight, *Islam from Within: Anthology of a Religion* (Belmont, CA: Wadsworth Publishers. Co., 1980), pp. 90–91.

16. *Original Sin*, pp. 83–103.

17. "The Story of Adam" (*Qissat Adam*), trans. and ed. Kenneth E. Nolin, *Muslim World*, LIV (1964), p.7.

18. "Man and His Perfection in Muslim Theology," *Muslim World*, XLIX (1959), pp. 22–23.

19. H. A. R. Gibb, "The Structure of Religious Thought in Islam," *Muslim World*, XXXVIII (1948), p. 28.

20. R. Arnaldez, "Ibn Hazm," *Encyclopaedia of Islam*, 2nd ed. (Leiden: E. J. Brill, 1960–), s.v.

21. A. J. Wensinck, *La Pensee de Ghazali* (Paris: Adrien-Maisonneuve, 1940), pp. 47–49. For this reference I am indebted to an unpublished paper of Ernest Hahn, "The Unforgivable Sin" (Toronto: Fellowship of Faith for Muslims, 1982).

22. *Ideals and Realities of Islam* (London: George Allen & Unwin, 1966), p. 38.

23. "Islamic Government Does Not Spend for Its Own Grandeur," *Kayhan International* (Sept. 4, 1985), p.3.

Chapter Three

DID JESUS DIE ON THE CROSS?
Reflections in Muslim Commentaries

Joseph L. Cumming
Yale University

INTRODUCTION

Did Jesus die on the cross and then rise from the dead? This question has re-markable power to generate vigorous discussion between Muslims and Chris-tians. As one contemporary writer has pointed out, "This subject, more than any other raises controversy among Muslims."[1] Indeed, whenever Muslims and Christians discuss religious matters together, the topic of conversation almost always seems to turn sooner or later to this question. Perhaps this is not surprising in light of a history in which the Crusades' exploitation of the cross as a religious symbol transformed it from a sign, which calls Christians to lay down their lives for others out of love,[2] into a sign of Christians' readi-ness to kill others for their own selfish ends.

Discussion of the crucifixion of Jesus generally leads to one of two con-clusions: (1) An effort by each side to persuade the other that "we are right and you are wrong," or (2) A polite decision to "agree to disagree." In either case this assumes that there is no common ground to be found on this ques-tion. It is the intent of this present paper to call that assumption into question. Specifically this paper will attempt a sympathetic examination of the Islamic tradition to see what answers to this question have been historically possible within the Muslim community. We will do this by examining the qur'anic verses which underlie the discussion, and the history of mainstream Sunni in-terpretation of these verses. A separate project (perhaps to be undertaken by a Muslim scholar?) would be to examine the Christian tradition in a similarly sympathetic way and then to consider what common ground may result from the two studies.

In the Muslim world today probably the most widely-known view on this question is that God caused someone else (a substitute) to appear to be Jesus, and that that substitute was crucified in Jesus' stead, while God took Jesus directly to heaven alive. Less well-known, but nonetheless widely held, is the view that Jesus himself was indeed nailed to the cross, but that he only lost consciousness on the cross and was subsequently revived in the tomb. This view, which has been popularized by the polemical writings of Ahmed Deedat, is most commonly found in South Asia today, where some groups assert that Jesus died a natural death many years later in Kashmir, where his tomb may be visited to this day.[3]

Both of these views (substitution and loss of consciousness) have historical support in the Islamic exegetical tradition, as do a number of other views as well. Islamic reflection on this question has historically centered on the exegesis of certain verses in the Qur'an. Though occasional remarks on the subject can be found in other genres, such as the *Rasā'il* of the *Ikhwān al-Safā'*,[4] the most influential Islamic discussion of the question is to be found in the tafsīr literature. It would be beyond the scope of this paper to attempt an encyclopedic analysis of all Islamic commentaries on this subject. In what follows we will focus on the most influential, mainstream commentaries of the Sunnī tradition. Specifically we will examine the commentaries of al-Tabari, Fakhr al-Dīn al-Rāzī, al-Baydāwī, and Sayyid Quṭb.[5]

These commentaries address the question of the death of Jesus in the context of exegeting four specific qur'ānic verses. I will list these verses here in translation. Much of the exegetical discussion focuses on the correct translation in these verses of the verb *tawaffā*. I will translate it according to its most common sense ("die"),[6] but I will place that translation in quotation marks to indicate that the word can be understood in other ways.

Āl 'Imrān [3]:55: [God said]: "O Jesus, I am causing you to 'die' [*mutawaffīka*] and raising you to myself, and cleansing you of those who do not believe, and causing those who follow you to be above those who do not believe until the Day of Resurrection.

Al-Nisā' [4]:157: [The Jews'] saying: "We killed Christ Jesus the son of Mary, the messenger of God." And they did not kill him, and they did not crucify him, but it was made to appear so to them [*shubbiha lahum*]. And those who have differed about it are in doubt about it: they do not have knowledge about it, but only the following of supposition. They did not kill him for certain.

Al-Mā'ida [5]:117: [Jesus said to God]: "I was a witness over them as long as I was among them, and when you caused me to 'die' [*tawaffaytanī*], you were their Overseer, and you are Witness over everything."

Maryam [19]:33: [Jesus said]: "Peace be upon me, the day I was born, the day I die [*amūtu*], and the day I am raised [*ub'athu*] alive."

In reference to the tradition of commentary on these verses, Roger Arnaldez expresses the following opinion:

> On voit que les commentaires sont loin de concorder. En particulier, la question se pose de savoir quand il faut situer la mort de Jésus. S'agit-il d'une mort au terme d'une vie humaine normale, ou d'une mort qui n'aura lieu que vers la fin des temps, quand viendra l'Heure dernière? Est-ce une mort véritable, ou une sorte de dormition? Et si c'est une mort véritable, coïncide-t-elle avec l'élévation au ciel, ou y a-t-il un intervalle entre les deux? Tous ces points ont été soutenus.[7]

In what follows we will see whether the commentary tradition is indeed as diverse as Arnaldez suggests. If so, then I would suggest that such broad diversity of interpretation should be seen not as a sign of a lack of concord, but rather of a rich exegetical heritage.

AL-TABARĪ

The first commentary which we will consider is that of Abū Ja'far Muhammad ibn Jarīr al-Tabarī (d. 310 A.H./923 A.D.). This is far from being the earliest commentary on the Qur'ān, but it is the earliest of the commentaries which still have profound and far-reaching influence on Muslims today. It is widely considered to be "*afdal al-tafāsīr al-ma'thūra al-jāmi'a li-aqwāl al-salaf fī al-tafsīr*"[8]—the highest example of a commentary which gathers the traditions and hadiths related to each verse, thus providing a window into how the Prophet and Companions and Followers may have interpreted the text. Though many of the isnāds are imperfect or incomplete (and al-Tabarī was aware of this), the traditions al-Tabarī reports provide, at the very least, an indication of the rich breadth and diversity of respectable Islamic exegesis in the third century A.H.

When dealing with verses which are open to multiple interpretations, al-Tabarī's frequent practice is to list, in order, each of the options which are represented in the traditions of which he is aware. Then, having listed all of these legitimate options, he frequently states which of them he considers to be "*rājih*," —most likely, or having the greater weight of evidence in its favor.

In his discussion of the meaning of *mutawaffī* in Āl 'Imrān [3]:55 we see an example of this kind of discussion. Al-Tabarī states:

> Exegetes [*ahl al-ta'wīl*] have differed about the meaning of the "death" [*wafāt*] of Jesus here:
>
> 1. Some of them have said: " 'Death' [*wafāt*] is with the meaning of sleep." The meaning for them is "I am causing you to sleep and raising you to myself in your sleep." . . .
>
> 2. Others have said, " 'Death' [*wafāt*] here is with the meaning of seizing [*qabd*]." The meaning is: "I am seizing you from the earth and raising you to myself." People commonly say: "I exacted [*tawaffaytu*] from so-and-so the money which he owed me." That is, I received it in full [*istawfaytuhu*] and I seized it [*qabadtuhu*]. So the meaning of His saying "I am causing you to 'die' and raising you to myself" is: I am seizing you from the earth alive to be close to me, and taking you to be with me without death, and raising you from among the unbelievers. . . .
>
> 3. Others have said, " 'Death' [*wafāt*] means the death of real, literal dying [*wafāt mawt ḥaqīqiyya*], that is, "I am causing you to die literally [*mumītuka*]." . . .
>
> 4. Others have said that this verse contains non-chronological arrangement [*taqdīm wa-ta'khīr*]. The implication is: I am raising you to myself and cleansing you of the unbelievers, and I will cause you to die after I send you back to earth at the end of time. . . . And the best-supported [*rājiḥ*] is the second statement: "I am seizing you [*qābiduka*] from the earth and causing you to 'die' [*mutawaffī ka*]." This is the best-supported [*rājiḥ*] because of the continuous transmission [*tawātur*] of reports from the Messenger of God (may God bless him and save him) about the return to earth of Jesus (upon him peace) at the end of time.[9]

Thus, al-Tabarī lists four theories of interpretation which he found in the traditions of Islamic exegesis before him: (1) sleep, (2) *wafāt = qabd*, (3) literal death, and (4) non-chronological arrangement. It is clear that he considers the second theory to have the best support in the traditions of which he is aware. But it is equally clear that he recognizes all four theories as having legitimate support in the traditions of Islamic exegesis of this text. The "sleep" theory may underlie the present-day view noted above according to which Jesus lost consciousness on the cross and revived in the tomb.

In his discussion of al-Nisā' [4]:157, al-Tabarī introduces the substitution theory (also noted above). Again here he is aware of traditions supporting multiple theories for interpreting this verse. He writes:

> How did God cause Jesus to appear to them? Exegetes have differed as to the manner of appearing which was caused to appear to the Jews in the matter of Jesus (upon him peace).[10]

Following the same system as before, al-Tabarī then lists multiple theories
for how this "causing to appear" took place. He is aware of a tradition which
holds that God caused the appearance of Jesus to fall upon all of his disciples
[*hawāriyyūn*], so that the Jews were unable to tell which of them was Jesus.
Al-Tabarī is also aware of a tradition which holds that Jesus asked his disciples for a single volunteer who would receive the appearance of Jesus and be
crucified in his place.

FAKHR AL-DĪN AL-RĀZĪ

If al-Tabarī is seen as the pinnacle of *tafsīr bi-l-ma'thūr*, the commentary of
Fakhr al-Dīn al-Rāzī (d. 606 A.H./1210 A.D.)[11] is widely seen as the pinnacle
of *tafsīr bi-l-ra'y*. Al-Rāzī does review the various interpretations enunciated
by his predecessors, and he does cite the traditions passed on from the
Prophet and Companions and Followers. But unlike al-Tabarī he does not always consider it necessary to repeat the isnads which support these traditions.
And, once he has reviewed the available options, his "brilliant, analytical
and questioning mind"[12] goes on to evaluate their theological significance. In
addition to his broad knowledge of the sciences of ḥadīth and tafsīr, al-Rāzī
was a brilliant theologian [*mutakallim*] with wide-ranging expertise in philosophy and a strong commitment to defending Ash'arite orthodoxy against
Mu'tazilism and other sects. Al-Rāzī brings all of this erudition to bear on his
discussion of the death of Jesus.

He begins by dividing the methods of exegeting the expression "I am causing you to 'die' [*mutawaffīka*]" (Āl 'Imrān [3]:55) into those which do *not* require chronological transposition [*taqdīm wa-ta'khīr*] of the "dying" and the
"raising", and those which *do*. It is clear that he prefers the former (which he
calls the "outward, evident sense [*zāhir*]"), and he addresses this first. He lists
eight different ways in which the expression can be understood, clearly im-
plying that he considers all eight to be legitimate:

1. The meaning of his saying "I am causing you to 'die' [*mutawaffīka*]," that
   is, bringing your lifespan to completion [*mutammim 'umrika*] and there-
   upon I will cause you to 'die' [*atawaffāka*]. I will not let them get as far as
   killing you, but I will raise you to my heaven and bring you near to my angels, and I will preserve you from their being able to kill you. This is a
   good interpretation.
2. "I am causing you to 'die' [*mutawaffīka*]," that is, causing your literal
   death [*mumītuka*]. And this is a tradition recounted on the authority of
   [*marwī 'an*] Ibn 'Abbās and Muḥammad ibn Isḥāq. They said: the purpose

was that his Jewish enemies should not be able to kill him, so then after that he honored him by raising him to heaven. Then, there are three different senses in which they understood this: First: Wahb said, "He died [*tuwuffiya*] for three hours, then was raised [*rufi'a*]." Second: Muḥammad ibn Isḥāq said, "He died [*tuwuffiya*] for seven hours, then God restored him to life [*aḥyāhu*] and raised him [rafa'*ahu*]." Third: al-Rabī' ibn Anas said, "He (exalted is he) caused him to die [*tawaffāhu*] at the moment when he raised him [*rafa'ahu*] to heaven." God has said (exalted is he) [in al-Zumar (39):42], "God causes souls to die [*yatawaffā al-anfus*] at the time of their death [*mawt*], and in their sleep those who have not died [*lam tamut*]."

3. In the interpretation of this verse, the "and" in his statement "causing you to 'die' and raising you to myself" does indicate chronological order. The verse proves that God (exalted is he) is the agent who does these actions to Jesus. But as for *how* he does them and *when* he does them, judgment must be suspended until there is proof. What does have clear proof is that Jesus is alive now. . . .

4. One interpretation, that of Abū Bakr al-Wāsiṭī, is that what is intended is "I am causing you to 'die' [*mutawaffīka*] to your desires and to the gratifications of your soul [*ḥuẓūẓ nafsika*]. Then he said "and raising you to myself." This is because whoever does not become annihilated in relation to all that is not God [*man lam yaṣir fāniyᵃⁿ 'ammā siwā Allāh*] will not attain the stage [*maqām*] of knowledge of God. Also, when Jesus was raised to heaven, he became like the angels, with the cessation of desire and of anger and of blameworthy morals.

5. *Al-tawaffī* means taking a thing in its totality [*wāfiyᵃⁿ*]. Since God knew that there were some people who would think that what God raised was Jesus' spirit, not his body, he mentioned these words to prove that Jesus (upon him blessing and peace) was raised in his entirety [*bi-tamāmihī*] to heaven, with both his spirit and his body. . . .

6. "I am causing you to 'die' [*mutawaffīka*]," that is, I will cause you to be like a dead man [*ka-l-mutawaffī*]. For if someone is raised to heaven and every trace of him is cut off from the earth, then he is like a dead man. Calling a thing by the name of something that resembles it in most of its characteristics and attributes is permissible and good.

7. *Al-tawaffī* means seizing [*al-qabd*]. People commonly say "So-and-so paid me back [*waffānī*] my money and repaid me in full [*awfānī*], and I exacted it [*tawaffaytuhā*] from him. . . .

8. This expression is elliptical, omitting an implied word: "causing your work to 'die'" with the meaning of receiving your work in full, and "raising you to myself" with the meaning of raising your work to myself. . . .

What is intended by this verse is that God (exalted is he) informed Jesus that he accepted his obedience and his works. . . .

This is a complete list of the different senses in which this verse is interpreted by those who take it according to its outward, evident sense [*'alā zāhirihā*].[13]

Al-Rāzī clearly considers all of the above to be legitimate options for interpretation within the Muslim community. Among them are some of the options which we have previously seen, such as:

1. actual, literal death and resurrection (#2 above), and
2. *wafāt = qabd* (#7 above).

There are also some interesting options which we have not previously seen, including:

1. Bringing an end to your lifespan (#1 above),
2. Agnosticism as to when and how the 'dying' and raising take place (#3 above),
3. Taking totally in body and spirit (#5 above), and
4. The Sūfī interpretation of al-Wāsiṭī that what is intended is a death to self and to carnal desires (#4 above).

Al-Rāzī also devotes considerable space to the substitution theory in connection with both Āl 'Imrān [3]: 55 and al-Nisā' [4]:157. He seems to feel that some kind of substitution is the most natural way to understand al-Nisā' [4]:157.[14] But he thinks that the substitution theory must answer some fairly serious grammatical and theological objections.

In his comments on al-Nisā' [4]:157 al-Rāzī presents the grammatical objection as follows:

> What is the grammatical subject of the verb *shubbiha*? If you say that its subject is Christ, [this will not work because] he is not supposed to have been made to resemble someone else: he is the one whom someone else is supposed to have been made to resemble! [*huwa al-mushabbah bi-hī wa-laysa bi-mushabbah*] And if you say that its subject is the one who was killed, [this will not work] because there is no mention [in the text] of the one who was killed [so he cannot serve as grammatical antecedent to the verb *shubbiha*].

There are two possible answers:

1. The verb's referent is the preposition and the object of the preposition [*al-jārr wa-l-majrūr*, i.e. the term "*lahum*"]. This is like the common expres-

sion "*khuyyila ilayhi*" ("he imagined", or "it appeared to him"). So it is as though the text said "[They did not kill him, and they did not crucify him,] but confusion befell them."

2. The subject of the verb is the [unexpressed] pronoun referring to the one who was killed, since God's saying "they did not kill him" indicates that killing happened to someone other than him, and that other person is "mentioned" in this way. So it is legitimate to make him the subject of *shubbiha*.[15]

It is worth noting that though answer #2 above presupposes that a substitution did take place, answer #1 does not. Answer #1 sees *shubbiha* as an impersonal passive meaning simply: "it appeared so to them" or "it was obscure/doubtful to them."

Continuing his comments on al-Nisā' [4]:157, al-Rāzī then presents his chief theological objection to the substitution theory and attempts to answer it:[16]

> If it were permissible to say that God (exalted is he) casts the appearance of one person onto another person, then this would open the door to sophistry. For if I see Zayd, perhaps it is not Zayd at all, but rather the appearance of Zayd has been cast onto this person! In that case neither marriage nor divorce nor property could continue to exist and be trusted. It would also lead to calling into question the idea of transmission of historical reports [*al-tawātur*] because a report which is historically transmitted can contribute to knowledge only on condition that its ultimate source is something perceptible to the senses. If we allow this kind of confusion to take place in things perceptible to the senses, then it will discredit historical transmission, and that will necessarily call into question all laws [*sharā'i'*].

One cannot reply to this objection that such things took place only in the time of the prophets (upon them blessing and peace); for we say that if what you have said is true, then that can only be known by evidence and proof. Anyone who does not know that evidence and that proof cannot assert anything with certainty on the basis of things perceptible to the senses, nor can he depend on any historically transmitted reports. Furthermore, even if in our day prophetic miracles [*mu'jizāt*] are blocked, the way of *karāmāt* [miraculous signs of divine favor] is still open. So the aforementioned possibility is still present in all ages. In sum: opening this door would of necessity discredit factual historical transmission. And discrediting that would of necessity discredit the prophethood of all prophets (upon them blessing and peace). So this branch would of necessity discredit the very roots. And *that* must be rejected.

The answer: The various schools of thought among scholars [*madhāhib al-'ulamā'*] have differed about this situation. They have mentioned several different interpretations: [Here al-Rāzī lists five versions of the substitution theory of which he is aware:

1. The Jews deliberately crucified another person and lied about it,
2. A man named Tītāyus was sent by "Judas the chief of the Jews" to kill Jesus, but God caused Tītāyus to appear like Jesus, and he was crucified instead,
3. The man charged with guarding Jesus was caused to look like Jesus and was crucified in his place,
4. Jesus asked his twelve disciples for a volunteer, and one man volunteered and was made to look like Jesus and was crucified,
5. A hypocritical disciple who proposed to betray Jesus was caused to look like Jesus and was crucified.

Al-Rāzī's summarizes in the following words his opinion of these answers to the objection: These interpretations are mutually contradictory and incompatible with one another. God knows best what the facts are about these matters![17]

Of all of the commentators whom this paper considers, Fakhr al-Dīn al-Rāzī has by far the most detailed, accurate and interesting analysis of what eastern Christians believed about the death and resurrection of Christ. Both his analysis of Christian beliefs and his own comments on those beliefs are worth quoting at length. In his discussion of al-Nisā' [4]:157, immediately following the discussion above, he discusses the statement in this verse that "those who have differed about it [i.e. the crucifixion] are in doubt about it." He considers whether this refers to the Jews or to the Christians, and he has the following to say about the Christians:

> All of the families of the Christians agree that the Jews killed him, but the largest groupings of Christians are three: the Nestorians, the Melkites[18] and the Jacobites.[19] Regarding the Nestorians, they claim that Christ was crucified with respect to his humanity, not with respect to his divinity. The view of most philosophers [*ḥukamā'*] is close to this statement. They say: Since it is established that a human being is not equivalent to this temple [i.e. the physical body], but is either a noble substance [*jism*] poured into this body [*badan*] or a spiritual/divine substance [*jawhar rūḥānī*] bare in its essence [*dhāt*] and conducting its affairs in this body [*badan*], thus the killing happened rather to this temple. As for the soul—which was in reality Jesus (upon him peace)—the killing did not happen to him.
>
> One should not say, "Every human being is like this, so what meaning does this distinction have?" For we say that Jesus' soul was holy, high, heavenly, strong in illumination [*ishrāq*] with the divine lights [*al-anwar al-ilāhiyya*],

great in closeness to the spirits of the angels. And when the soul is like that, its suffering because of death and the destruction of the body [*badan*] is not great. And after it has been separated from the shade of the body, it will escape to the wide expanse of the heavens and the lights of the world of glory. Its joy and happiness there will be great. And it is known that these states do not occur in all people. From the beginning of the creation of Adam (upon him peace) until the consummation of the Day of Resurrection, they do not occur except with a few individuals. This is the significance of distinguishing Jesus (upon him peace) in this way.

Regarding the Melkites, they say: the killing and the crucifixion happened to [*waṣalā ilā*] the divinity in sense and in feeling, not in direct experience [*bi-l-mubāshara*]. And the Jacobites say: the killing and the crucifixion happened to Christ, who is a substance resulting from two substances [*jawhar mutawallid min jawharayn*]. This is an explanation of the teachings of the Christians on this subject.[20]

In a 1980 article, Mahmoud Ayoub suggests that al-Rāzī's comments here are an outstanding example of what he calls "the Qur'ānic spirit of conciliation and search for meaning beyond the mere facts of history."[21] He adds:

[Al-Rāzī's] statement goes a long way towards meeting the Qur'ānic challenge of Jesus, the Christ. It also provides a good starting point for Muslim-Christian understanding.[22]

Incidentally, al-Rāzī's suggestion that Jesus has a dual nature—spiritual/heavenly [*rūḥānī*] and physical/earthly [*badanī*] is not solely a late, Hellenizing innovation with no roots in authentically Islamic soil. The germ of this idea can be found in Ibn Isḥāq—the earliest biographer of Muḥammad, to whom al-Rāzī referred earlier. Ibn Isḥāq wrote that after Jesus instructed his disciples to carry God's commands to the whole world,

Then God raised him to Him and garbed him in feathers and dressed him in light and cut off his desire for food and drink, so he flew among the angels, and he was with them around the throne. He was human and angelic, heavenly and earthly.[23]

AL-BAYDĀWĪ

The Qur'ān commentary of Nāṣir al-Dīn Abū Saʿīd ʿAbdallāh al-Baydāwī (d. 685 A.H./1286 A.D. or 691 A.H./1291 A.D.) is one of the most influential in the world today. This is partly because of its relatively handy size, but it is also because al-Baydāwī's commentary made use of the brilliant philological and grammatical erudition in al-Zamakhsharī's commentary *al-Kashshāf*. However, al-Baydāwī edited out al-Zamakhsharī's Muʿtazilite tendencies and so produced a commentary of impeccable Sunnī Ashʿarite orthodoxy. Yet it would be a mistake to imply that al-Baydāwī did nothing more than rework the *Kashshāf*. Al-Baydāwī was clearly also familiar with the other Sunnī commentaries which had preceded his own.

In keeping with his crisp, handbook-like style, al-Baydāwī frequently simply lists all of the various legitimate interpretations of a given verse, without indicating either the origin of each option or which of them he prefers. Such is the case with his comments on Āl ʿImrān (3):55:[24]

"O Jesus, I am causing you to 'die' [*mutawaffīka*]." That is,

1. Bringing an end to your lifespan and bringing you to the appointed end of your lifespan, protecting you from their killing, or
2. Seizing you [*qābiduka*] from the earth, as in the expression "I exacted [*tawaffaytu*] my money," or
3. Causing you to 'die' [*mutawaffīka*] sleeping, since it is recounted [*ruwiya*] that he raised him sleeping, or
4. Causing you to die [*mumītuka*] to the desires which hinder you from ascending to the world of the heavenly realm, and
5. It is said that God literally caused him to die [*amātahu*] for seven hours and then [*thumma*] raised him to heaven. And this is the view of the Christians.[25]

Thus al-Baydāwī lists as legitimate interpretations several of the theories we have already seen: (1) ending your lifespan, (2) *wafāt* = *qabd*, (3) sleep, (4) death to earthly desires, and (5) actual, literal death and resurrection.

On al-Māʾida [5]:117 al-Baydāwī comments:

"When you caused me to 'die' [*tawaffaytanī*]," i.e., by raising to heaven, in accordance with His saying "I am causing you to 'die' [*mutawaffīka*] and raising you." The verb *tawaffā* means to take something totally [*wāfiyᵃⁿ*], and death [*al-mawt*] is one kind of this. God (exalted is He) says: "God causes souls to 'die' [*yatawaffā al-anfus*] at the time of their death [*mawt*], and in their sleep those who have not died."[26]

In his discussion of al-Nisāʾ [4]:157 al-Baydāwī also mentions a group of people [*qawm*] (the context suggests that they are Christians or Jews, not Muslims) who hold the view that "the human nature [*nāsūt*] was crucified and the divine nature [*lāhūt*] ascended."[27]

Al-Baydāwī is also aware of the substitution theory and of the traditions which support it. In his comments on al-Nisāʾ [4]:157 he reports two versions of the substitution theory: (1) Jesus asked the disciples for a volunteer to take his place when he knew that the Jews were coming to kill him in revenge for God's having turned a band of Jewish revilers into apes and pigs, or (2) a Jew named Tītānus was the victim. In addition to these two versions of the substitution story, al-Bayḍāwī adds that he knows of stories of "other similar unusual miracles [*khawāriq*] which would not be inconceivable [*lā tustab'adu*] in the age of the prophets."[28]

Nevertheless al-Bayḍāwī raises two serious problems with the substitution theory. The first problem is theological, having to do with how one may properly predicate deceit as an attribute of God; and the second problem is grammatical, having to do with commentators' confusion over the subject of the passive verb *shubbiha*.

In commenting on Āl 'Imrān [3]:54, al-Bayḍāwī argues the following:

> Deception [*al-makr*], insofar as it is (at the root) a ruse which brings harm to another person, cannot be predicated of God [*lā yusnadu ilā Allāh*] (exalted is he), except by way of requital and reciprocity [*al-muqābala wa-l-izdiwāj*].[29]

For this reason al-Bayḍāwī thinks that any substitution theory, in order to be plausible, must necessarily assume that the person who was crucified was himself guilty of "seeking to kill Jesus [*qaṣada ightiyālahu*]."[30] Of course this objection does not require al-Bayḍāwī to reject the substitution theory *as such*, but it does imply a rejection of the large majority of the traditional *versions* of that theory (including those with relatively stronger isnāds), in which an innocent man (one of Jesus' disciples, or Sergius, or Simon of Cyrene, or an anonymous passer-by, etc.) was unjustly crucified as a result of the deception. The versions in which a guilty man like Judas Iscariot was crucified have relatively weak support in the ḥadīth.

Incidentally Mahmoud Ayoub agrees with this critique of the substitution theory. He adds:

> The substitutionist theory will not do, regardless of its form or purpose. First, it makes a mockery of divine justice and the primordial covenant of God with humanity, to guide human history to its final fulfillment.[31] Would it be in consonance with God's covenant, his mercy and justice, to deceive humanity for so many centuries?[32] . . . It makes historical Christianity based on a divine deception which was not disclosed until the Qur'ān was revealed centuries later.[33]

Al-Bayḍāwī's second objection to the substitution theory is grammatical. In commenting on al-Nisā' [4]:157 ("it was made to appear so to them" [*shubbiha lahum*]), after reporting two versions of the substitution story, he argues:

> The verb *shubbiha* is a grammatical predicate referring to [*musnad ilā*] the preposition and the object of the preposition [*al-jārr wa-l-majrūr*], as though it

said "confusion [*tashbīh*] befell them between Jesus and the person killed," or "confusion befell them in the matter." This accords with the statement of those who say that "No one was killed, but a false rumor arose and spread among the people."[34]

Al-Baydāwī is echoing here a grammatical argument previously made by al-Zamakhsharī,[35] and it is essentially the same as the grammatical objection raised by al-Rāzī. Al-Zamakhsharī argues along the following lines: The verb *shubbiha* must be an impersonal passive. If the subject of this passive verb were Jesus, then it would mean that Jesus was caused to resemble someone else. But that is the reverse of what the substitution stories relate: Jesus was not caused to resemble someone else; someone else is supposed to have been made to resemble Jesus.[36] And the subject of the passive verb *shubbiha* cannot be the substitute who was killed [*al-maqtūl*], because that person is not mentioned in the Qur'ān, so cannot serve grammatically as an antecedent subject. Therefore *shubbiha*, as grammatical predicate, must refer to the preposition "to" and its object "them" [*lahum*]. It must be an impersonal passive meaning "they were made to imagine it," or "the matter was made to appear so to them," or "the matter was made obscure/doubtful to them." Al-Baydāwī's brief grammatical remarks, quoted above, are a condensation of this argument of al-Zamakhsharī.

In view of al-Baydāwī's grammatical and theological objections to the substitution theory, one wonders what "tone of voice" or nuance he intended behind his remark that the various and diverse substitution stories describe "unusual miracles which would not be inconceivable in the age of the prophets" [*al-khawāriq al-latī lā tustab'adu fī zamān al-nubuwwa*]. Certainly such supernatural acts are not inconceivable: God is *able* to do them. But, in reading stories according to which God turned Jewish enemies into apes and pigs or caused seventeen disciples all to look and sound identically like Jesus while Jesus flew through an aperture which opened in the roof, perhaps al-Baydāwī wondered whether it is plausible that God *would* do such a thing, in view of what the Qur'ān says elsewhere about God's character. Al-Tabarī's editor does not hesitate to state that some of these kinds of hadiths are spurious "fables" [*asāṭīr*].[37]

SAYYID QUṬB

Sayyid Quṭb wrote what is perhaps the most widely-known Sunnī commentary of the twentieth century. It has been very influential despite (or perhaps because of) the author's lack of formal theological training at al-Azhar. A leader of the Muslim Brothers [*al-Ikhwān al-Muslimūn*] until his execution at the hands of the Egyptian government in 1966, he was clearly more concerned to refute the errors of Christianity than to seek common theological ground with Christians.[38] He is vigorous in denouncing Christian "deification" of Jesus.

When it comes to the crucifixion of Jesus, however, he insists on agnosticism. This certainly does not mean that he would be prepared to attribute any redemptive significance to Jesus' death and rising if they did actually take place. But he does insist that the historical question is an open one, and that we cannot know for certain the "when" or "how" of Jesus' death and rising.

In taking this position, he echoes another modern commentary, Rashīd Ridā's *Tafsīr al-Manār*. Rashīd Ridā writes an extended polemic in which he refutes the Christian theological view that Jesus' death and resurrection atoned for the sins of the world, reconciling divine justice and divine mercy. He is clear, however, that his dispute with Christians is over the theological significance which they attribute to the crucifixion, not over the historical event itself. Thus he writes, "The actual fact of the crucifixion is not itself a matter which the Book of God seeks to affirm or deny, except for the purpose of asserting the killing of prophets by the Jews unjustly, and reproaching them for that act."[39]

Sayyid Quṭb takes a similarly agnostic view on the historical question of when and how Jesus "died" and rose. Commenting on Āl 'Imrān [3]:55, he writes:

> As for how his "death" [*wafāt*] came about, and how his being raised came about, these are mysterious matters [*umūr ghaybiyya*] which fall into the category of obscure verses [*mutashābihāt*] whose exegesis no one knows but God. There is no use in trying to get to the bottom of them, either in doctrine or in law. Those who chase after them and make them into a matter for dispute will only end up falling into a state of doubt and confusion and complexity, without coming to any certainty in truth and without being able to rest their minds in a matter which must be entrusted to the knowledge of God.[40]

Commenting on al-Nisā' [4]:157, he says that "the Jews say that they killed him[41] . . . and the Christians say that Jesus was crucified and buried and rose from the dead after three days, and 'history'[42] is silent about the birth of Christ and his end."[43] Sayyid Quṭb argues that it is impossible to be certain about these things.

Sayyid Quṭb then reviews the New Testament accounts on the subject, using the interesting terminology "*yarwī*" (recounts), "*riwāya*" (account), "*khabar*" (report) and "*tarjuḥu*" (is more probable, has more support). This is the same terminology which the classical commentators (see al-Ṭabarī above, for example) use to refer to Islamic traditional accounts attributed to the

Prophet, Companions and Followers. Implicitly he seems to treat the New Testament text as being in the category of ḥadīth whose reliability should be assessed on the basis of its chain of transmission from the apostolic generation.

He casts doubt on the isnād of the New Testament accounts, suggesting that the accounts which Christians have accepted as canonical were chosen for "reasons which are not above doubt."[44] But he does not absolutely reject the New Testament accounts as false. He also mentions the contrasting story in the so-called "Gospel of Barnabas,"[45] but he does not attempt to assess whether "Barnabas" constitutes a reliable account. The main point which he wishes to underline is what he states as his conclusion on the matter:

> Thus the scholar cannot find any certain report [khabar yaqīn] about this event . . . nor can those who differ about it find any support which would make one account [riwāya] more plausible [yurajjiḥu] over another account [riwāwa].[46]

He then turns to his interpretation of the Qur'ān's statement in al-Nisā' [4]:158 that God "raised" Jesus [rafa'ahu]:

> The Qur'ān does not offer details about this raising. Was it a raising of both body and spirit in a state of being alive? Or was it a raising of the spirit only after death [wafāt]? And when did this death [wafāt] take place, and where? They did not kill him, and they did not crucify him; rather the killing and the crucifixion happened to someone who was obscure to them [man shubbiha lahum] without him. The Qur'ān does not offer any other details behind this fact, except what appears in His saying (exalted is He) "O Jesus, I am causing you to 'die' [mutawaffīka] and raising you to myself." This verse, like the one we have been discussing, does not give details about the death [wafāt], nor about the nature of this 'dying' [tawaffī] and its timing. In keeping with our method, "in the shelter of the Qur'ān,"[47] we do not wish to come out from under that shelter, nor to wander about in sayings and fables for which we have no proof.[48]

In his discussion of al-Mā'ida [5]:117 Sayyid Quṭb again expresses agnosticism, but seems to suggest more clearly that he is inclined to think that Jesus really did die and rise. He writes:

> The outward, evident meaning [zāhir] of the qur'ānic texts indicates [yufīdu] that God (exalted is he) caused Jesus son of Mary to die [tawaffā], and then [thumma] raised him to Himself. Some traditions [al-āthār] indicate [tufīdu] that he is alive with God. As far as I can see, there is no contradiction which would raise any problem between the idea that God caused him to die [tawafāhu] from the life of the earth and the idea that he is alive with Him. After all, martyrs similarly die on earth and are alive with God. As to what form their life

with Him takes, we do not know any "how" about it [*lā nadrī lahā kayf^(an)*]. Similarly we do not know what form the life of Jesus (upon him peace) takes.[49]

Sayyid Quṭb is apparently alluding here to the qur'ānic command in al-Baqara (2):154: "Do not say of those who are killed in the service of God, 'They are dead.' Rather, they are living, but you do not perceive." And in Āl 'Imrān [3]:169: "Do not consider those who have been killed in the service of God to be dead. Rather, they are alive with their Lord."

In his comments on Maryam [19]:33 Sayyid Quṭb writes:

> The text is unequivocal [*ṣarīḥ*] here regarding the death [*mawt*] and resurrection [*ba'th*] of Jesus. It leaves no room for explaining-away [*ta'wīl*] or for dispute.

CONCLUSION

Did Jesus die on the cross and then rise from the dead? The foregoing discussion and analysis show what a rich and diverse range of answers to this question have historically been seen as legitimately supported within the Muslim community. Throughout the centuries there has never been just one, single "correct" Islamic answer to the question of whether Jesus died on the cross. Indeed, as the wide-ranging and erudite reflections of the commentators have shown, it is not just a simple "yes-or-no" question. Among the varied answers which Muslims have given through the centuries, I believe that there is much more room to find common ground with Christians than is generally supposed by either Muslims or Christians today.

A partial list of the interpretations which we have found in the major commentaries includes the following:

1. The substitution theory,
2. The sleep theory (including loss of consciousness on the cross),
3. *wafāt* = *qabḍ* (with various interpretations of what God "seized" and when),
4. Chronological transposition, with eschatological death and resurrection,
5. God "brought an end to Jesus' earthly lifespan,"
6. God "took Jesus totally, in body and soul,"
7. Agnosticism as to when and how the dying and rising take place
8. The Sūfī challenge of death to self and to carnal desires,
9. "Like the martyrs, Jesus died a real death, but is alive with God," and
10. Real, literal death and resurrection.

Of course these interpretations are not all mutually exclusive. For example, one might hold #3, #5 and #6 simultaneously as different ways of saying the same thing.

What implications does this have for Muslim-Christian dialogue? Option #10 will of course be readily seen as having common ground with Christians. But #3, #5, #6, and #9 all might also be understood in ways that might suggest common ground. These might serve as starting-points for Muslim-Christian dialogue on the question.

Particularly intriguing is al-Rāzī's tentative exploration of the idea that Jesus had an earthly nature which died on the cross and a heavenly nature which suffered death only with regard to its union with the earthly nature. I agree with Mahmoud Ayoub's suggestion that this constructive effort by al-Rāzī might make an excellent starting-point for discussion between Muslims and Christians.[50]

In any case it should be clear that there is plenty of room to explore common ground in the multiple different interpretation options which the Muslim commentary tradition has preserved throughout the centuries. This rich and diverse exegetical heritage invites us to embark upon that exploration.

NOTES

1. Iskandar Jadīd, *Al-Salīb fī al-Injīl wa-l-Qur'ān* (Beirut: Markaz al-Shabība, n.d.), p. 5.

2. Cf. 1 John 3:16 or Philippians 2:4–8, for example.

3. Kenneth Cragg, *The Call of the Minaret,* second edition, revised and enlarged (Ibadan: Daystar Press, 1985), p. 224.

4. Neal Robinson, *Christ in Islam and Christianity* (Albany: State University of New York Press, 1991), pp. 56-57 summarizes the view of the *Ikhwān al-Safān'* thus: "Jesus' humanity (*nās ūt*) was crucified, and his hands were nailed to the cross. He was left there all day, given vinegar to drink, and pierced with a lance. He was taken down from the cross, wrapped in a shroud and laid in the tomb. Three days later he appeared to the disciples and was recognized by them. When the news spread that he had not been killed, the Jews opened up the tomb but did not find his mortal remains (*nās ūt*). Although the Brethren of Purity rejected Christian claims concerning Christ's divinity, they appear to have been reconciled to belief in the reality of the crucifixion."

5. An earlier edition of this paper included also an analysis of the commentary of Abū 'Abdallāh al-Qurṭubī (d. 671/1272) on this subject, but that section of this paper had to be cut for reasons of length. I would be happy to make this material available to anyone who is interested. Admittedly Sayyid Quṭb is in some ways out of the mainstream, but there is no question that his Qur'ān commentary has been very influential in the twentieth century.

6. Robinson, op. cit., p. 118.

7. *Jésus: Fils de Marie, prophète de l'Islam* (Paris : Desclée, 1980), pp. 190–191.

8. Salāḥ 'Abd al-Fattāḥ al-Khālidī, Introduction to Abū Ja'far Muḥammad ibn Jarīr al-Tabarī, *Tafsīr al-Tabarī: Jāmi' al-Bayān 'an Ta'wīl Āy al-Qur'ān* (Damascus: Dār al-Qalam, 1997), vol. 1, p. 6.

9. Al-Tabarī, *Tafsīr*, pp. 10–11.

10. Ibid., loc. cit.

11. Jane Dammen McAuliffe, *Qur'anic Christians: An Analysis of Classical and Modern Exegesis* (Cambridge: Cambridge University Press, 1991), p. 66n.151 insists that 1209 is incorrect.

12. Mahmoud Ayoub, "Towards an Islamic Christology, II: The Death of Jesus, Reality or Delusion (A Study of the Death of Jesus in Tafsīr Literature)," in *The Muslim World*, vol. LXX, No. 2 (Hartford: The Hartford Seminary Foundation, April, 1980), p. 92.

13. Muḥammad Fakhr al-Dīn ibn al-'Allāma Diyā' al-Dīn 'Umar Al-Rāzī, *Tafsīr al-Fakhr al-Rāzī, al-Mushtahir bi-l-Tafsīr al-Kabīr wa-Mafātīḥ al-Ghaib*, Khalīl Muhyī al-Dīn al-Mais (ed.) (Beirut: Dar al-Fikr, 1990), *s.v.* "Āl 'Imrān (3):55."

14. In his comments on Al 'Imran [3]:55 he says, "The text of the Qur'ān indicates [*yadullu 'alā*] that when God (exalted is he) raised Jesus, he cast his appearance onto someone else." But in al-Rāzī's comments on al-Nisā' (4):157, as will be seen below, he seems less certain that this is the best way to interpret the verse.

15. Al-Rāzī, loc. cit.

16. He lists other objections and attempts to answer them in his comments on Āl 'Imrān (3):55.

17. Al-Rāzī, loc. cit.

18. That is, those who hold to the doctrine of the official Byzantine church.

19. Muslim writers from this period used the term "Jacobite" as a catch-all term to describe all of the so-called "Monophysite" churches, not just the Syrian church which was loyal to the teaching of Jacob Baraddeus.

20. Al-Rāzī, loc. cit.

21. Mahmoud Ayoub, "Towards an Islamic Christology, II: The Death of Jesus, Reality or Delusion (A Study of the Death of Jesus in Tafsīr Literature)," in *The Muslim World*, vol. LXX, No. 2 (Hartford: The Hartford Seminary Foundation, April, 1980), p. 105.

22. Ibid.

23. Gordon Darnell Newby (ed.), *The Making of the Last Prophet : A Reconstruction of the Earliest Biography of Muhammad* (Columbia: University of South Carolina Press, 1989), p. 210.

24. I have added the numbers and paragraph breaks in this quotation.

25. Nāṣir al-Dīn abū Sa'īd 'Abdallāh ibn 'Umar ibn Muḥammad al-Shīrāzī al-Baydāwī, *Tafsīr al-Baydāwī al-Musammā Anwār al-Tanzīl wa-Asrār al-Ta'wīl* (Beirut: Dār al-Kutub al-'Ilmiyya, 1988), loc. cit.

26. Al-Baydāwī, loc. cit. The qur'ānic reference quoted is al-Zumar (39):42.

27. Ibid., loc. cit.

28. Ibid.

29. Ibid.
30. Ibid.
31. Ayoub has a footnote here: "S. 7:172; 2:38."
32. Ayoub, 1980, p. 104.
33. Ibid., p. 97.
34. Al-Baydāwī, loc. cit.
35. Mahmoud Ayoub, 1980, p. 101. I am dependent on Ayoub here for his summary of al-Zamakhsharī's grammatical argument.
36. I note, however that it *would* be consonant with the theory that Jesus lost consciousness on the cross and thus was caused to appear to die. It would also be consonant with the theory that Jesus did actually die on the cross, but that his death only appeared to be the result of the crucifixion, whereas in fact it was God who caused him to die. In this connection, note the theology of al-Anfāl (8):17: "You did not kill them, but God killed them, and you did not throw (your spear) when you threw, but rather God threw [*lam taqtulūhum wa-lākinna Allāh qatala, wa-māramayta idh ramayta wa-lākinna Allāh ramā*]."
37. Salāḥ 'Abd al-Fattāḥ al-Khālidī, Introduction to al-Tabarī, *Tafsīr*, vol. 1, p. 12 et passim.
38. I have watched on videotape a number of his lectures which were devoted to refutation of the "*inḥirāfāt*" of the Christians and the Jews, which he saw as a threat to the integrity of Islam.
39. Sayyid Muḥammad Rashīd Riḍā, *Tafsīr al-Manār* (Cairo: Dār al-*Manār*, 1367), 2nd edition, VI, p.18, cited in Mahmoud Ayoub (1980), op. cit., p. 114.
40. Ibrāhim Ḥusayn Shādhilī Sayyid Quṭb, *Fī Zilāl al-Qur'ān: ṭab'a jadīda mashrū'a tudamminu idāfāt wa-tanqīḥāt tarakahā al-mu'allif wa-tunsharu li-l-marra al-ūlā* (Beirut: Dār al-Mashriq, 1973), loc. cit.
41. An assertion that Jews today would certainly deny!
42. Quotation marks are his.
43. Sayyid Quṭb, ibid., loc. cit.
44. Ibid.
45. Mahmoud Ayyoub, in his 1980 article (op. cit.) p. 112, points out, "This is most probably a late work, written under Islamic influence." In fact it was almost certainly first penned by a Christian convert to Islam in the 14th century in Latin, and it contains quotations from Dante's *Divine Comedy*, but to review the evidence on this would be beyond the scope of this paper.
46. Sayyid Quṭb, op. cit.
47. This is the title of Sayyid Quṭb's whole commentary.
48. Sayyid Quṭb, op. cit.
49. Ibid., loc. cit. Note that Sayyid Quṭb penned these words about martyrs during an imprisonment which ended in his own execution.
50. Ayoub, 1980, p. 105.

Chapter Four

COVENANT COMMUNITY IN A DIVIDED WORLD

Ng Kam Weng
Director, Kairos Research Centre
Kuala Lumpur, Malaysia

I. THE SOCIAL IMPACT OF CHRISTIAN SALVATION

Introduction

Christians have commonly been described as the 'people of the Book'. The term rightly recognizes the centrality of the Bible in the faith and practice of Christians. Nevertheless, the term fails to spell out how the Bible provides Christians with a way of life that is centered around love for and obedience to God. For this reason, I prefer the term the 'people of the Covenant'. We have in the Bible the Old Covenant and the New Covenant. The New Covenant is anticipated in the Old Covenant and the Old Covenant is fulfilled in the New Covenant.

What is a Covenant? Sometimes it is understood as a treaty or an alliance between two parties ratified by treaty documents. The Bible indicates that the all-sufficient God took the initiative to establish a Covenant which includes special favors and protection to the people of the Covenant. The Covenant that the Bible describes goes beyond legal requirements since the two parties enter into a special relationship, pledging a mutual commitment of an intensely personal kind. Hence, loyalty and faithfulness are the central qualities of the biblical Covenant. As 1 Peter 2: 9–10 says, "You are a chosen people, a royal priesthood, a holy nation, a people belonging to God that you may declare the praises of him who called you out of darkness into his marvelous light. Once you were not a people, but now you are the people of God; once you had not received mercy, but now you have received the mercy of God."

It is evident that divine revelation goes beyond transmission of information. It has a more inclusive role of establishing a Covenant relationship. The relationship is ratified by the ritual of atoning sacrifice which emphasizes that sinful humans can enjoy the benefits of this Covenant only because God has provided the means to overcome/cover sin which has earlier caused estrangement between God and humanity. Finally, the Covenant includes a deposition of authoritative scriptures that spell out in detail the obligations entailed in keeping this relationship, which is a way of life characterized by utmost loyalty, trust and obedience to God.

By definition, an agreement involves at least two parties. It would be a very odd Covenant in which one party knows what the other party desires, but does not know who the other party really is. Just imagine entering a Covenant with someone via the Internet. The other party may offer me the sweetest deal along with wonderful promises, but I would not dream of entering into a Covenant with this person until I knew him or her personally. By the same token, the God of the Covenant does not put himself out to be a remote God. The God of the Bible not only reveals his will (often envisaged divine law) but also who he is and what he is like, that is, his personality. In other words, God not only sends messages through intermediaries like prophets, he also comes in the form of Jesus Christ, a personal revelation of God in human history. As the book of Hebrews testifies, "God, after he spoke to the fathers in the prophets in many portions and in many ways, in these last days has spoken to us in his Son, whom he appointed heir of all things, through whom also he made the world" (Heb. 1:1–2).

The goal of Revelation is not abstract knowledge but restoration of a (lost) relationship with God. Revelation creates a genuine (ontic) relationship in which the recipient is affirmed in a dialogical relationship with God. Ray Anderson writes, "In concrete social situations, only relationships which have the character of placing person into the truth of relation with God are considered normative, and is the standard by which all other concepts of personality are measured."[1] The Christian then sees a person as affirmed in the context of community. A person is only totally a person in community. The Christian rejects any atomistic concept of the person that isolates him or her from a larger community. Revelation is appropriated in the context of involvement, response, integration, that is to say, in the context of relationships.

Excursus: Speech-Act philosophy and the Nature of Language

J. L. Austin through his speech-act theory demonstrated that language is multi-dimensional. Vincent Brummer notes that in speaking we go beyond proposing a picture of reality (*constatives*). We also express convictions and attitudes (*expressives*), we commit ourselves before our hearers to some specific future act(s) (*commisives*) and we finally accept an obligation before our hearers (*prescriptives*).[2]

In the light of this speech-act philosophy, restricting Revelation to mean sending of divine commands presupposes a view of language that postulates a duality that separates the speaker from reality and from the persons he or she wishes to communicate with. In contrast, speech-act theory emphasizes that when a person uses language, he or she projects himself or herself into reality with the intention of changing it. Speech also creates a relationship between the speaker and the hearer. There is therefore no dichotomy between language (thought) and action (reality and relationship). Speech, then, is more than a cognitive intent, it involves the whole person. Jerry Gill emphasizes that the speaker gives his personal backing to his speech. "Thus *truth is a function of personal commitment*. There is a sense in which every statement must necessarily participate in both the factual and valuational dimensions simultaneously. Technically speaking, each statement should be prefaced by the phrase, "I say," thereby indicating the speaker's responsibility for making it."[3]

In the light of these recently philosophical insights into the nature of language we see the cogency of the Christian understanding of revelation which makes the primarily purpose of divine revelation as aiming towards establishing fellowship and eliciting a human response in the form of worship of a personal God.

Theological and Social Perspectives

Divine Accountability

It is the thesis of this paper that Christianity offers resources for social renewal. In particular, the biblical Covenant supports the creation of a community which embodies a way of life that upholds justice and integrity, emphasis on mutual accountability in the presence of a transcendental authority and peaceableness and hope in a world rent by tragic conflicts.

For this purpose, this paper attempts to give a descriptive analysis of some principles of building community as recorded in the Bible, describing how they have been developed and expressed historically among believers as the Covenant people of God. Hopefully their usefulness and relevance to our contemporary quest for community will be made evident in the process.

It is clear in the Bible that the origin of the community of faith is not deduced from a concept of a cosmos or timeless social order. Its origin lay in a collective experience of deliverance by a God who is both relational and dynamic in his action. In particular, the Covenant community through her collective memory – offers a constructive approach to society that stresses freedom and responsibility in the practice of law and ordering of society. The definitive event of the Exodus rejected the dominating and oppressive system in Pharaoh's Egypt as unjust and therefore illegitimate. Paul Hanson explains how the experience of deliverance profoundly gave rise to a unique worldview.

> Whereas the heavenly realm functioned within the dominant societies of that time to rationalize and stabilize the status quo, the fact that the Hebrew community was born out of a decisive break with the "eternal" social order of the pharaohs directed attention to the God who interacted with the human family within the stuff of history so as to replace oppressive structures with forms conducive to the well being of all creatures.[4]

The Covenant community is special not because it was numerous and powerful but because it was a community of law and order. For example in Deuteronomy 4:5–8 and 7:6–8, the Covenant community was reminded that her special position rested in the wisdom of the law which proved her God to be a unique and living God. Much of biblical law was concerned with the just ordering of society so that it reflected the righteous character of God. This law ensures that unity is grounded in mutual accountability before the one true God. Consequently, any misunderstanding of who God is leads to abuse of power and deformation of just social life.

Bruggemann observes that the Covenant community depends on a clear vision and a sharp memory of who God is.

> To forget God's radical character is to engage in idolatry, to imagine a God who is not so free, dangerous, powerful, or subversive as is the God of the exodus. . . . Within this community, every individual was equally precious to God, regardless of social standing and thus to be protected from exploitation and oppression by the structures intrinsic to the covenant between God and people.[5]

Neighborly Justice

The theme of solidarity recurs constantly in the Old Testament as the basic motive in building a caring and supportive community. Nevertheless, solidarity must not be confused with collectivism where the individual is sacrificed on the altar of social engineering. Sociality does not absorb individuality. Every person is held to be responsible both for his and her individual acts and for the acts of his community. Specifically, each member is expected to fulfill his or her obligation to maintain the covenantal social order. A religious vision leads to a struggle to secure a social arrangement congruent with that vision. On the other hand, the vision takes practical effect only in the context of a concrete social order.

Imitation of God requires the implementation of a legal system that protects the powerless and shows compassion towards the vulnerable (Deut. 16:20). Exaction of interest from the poor was prohibited (Ex. 22:25–27) and the poor hired servant must not be oppressed (Deut. 24:14–15). Kindness was to be extended even to the resident alien who must be treated with justice (Ex. 22:21–24). In sum, "You shall not pervert the justice due to the sojourner or to the fatherless, or take a widow's garment in pledge" (Deut. 24:17).

Other laws that reinforced the covenant justice can be seen in the law of inheritance which was primarily aimed at preventing monopoly and exploitation which results in a poverty trap and the social and economic displacement of the people. Proverbs 22:28–29 and 23:10–11 both prohibit the removal of landmarks indicating original owners of the land. Christopher Wright elaborates,

> The law requires the restoration of land to their original status and ownership and the release of those who were forced to sell themselves into slave labor due to poverty would be restored in the sabbatical year (seventh year) and jubilee year (fiftieth year). See Exodus 21:1–2; Leviticus 25 and Deuteronomy 15:1–18. The Jubilee attempts to reverse the downward spiral of debt and poverty and protects the economic sufficiency of the household in a family-oriented economy.[6]

Nevertheless, such laws require a sense of social responsibility and compassion for the welfare of the needy and weak rather than a set of demands enforced legalistically. That is to say, the Covenant assumes a social order held together by habits of neighborliness.

Inclusiveness

What happens if the Covenant community becomes a minority within a larger secular society? Under such circumstances, implementations of the ideals to wider society are not given up. Submission to superior ruling powers must not lead to abandonment of the self-identity of the community. Interestingly, the secular authorities were seen as limited but relatively legitimate. Some specific responses include the following.

1. God's people were urged to *pray* for the rulers and even seek their welfare (Jer. 29).
2. God's people should be ready to offer service with integrity under secular governments for the common good so long as religious integrity is not compromised (Book of Daniel).

3. The religious identity of believers was to be nurtured by renewed dedication to the laws of the Covenant.
4. Religious devotion must seek to sustain hope in God's final deliverance and vindication of the believing community.

In this regard, both Daniel and Joseph served as exemplars on how to serve fruitfully under an unbelieving authority. Believers should try to influence and shape public policy for the welfare of the economically deprived and socially marginalized. Ezra and Nehemiah suggest the remarkable possibility and indeed the responsibility of believing officials to avail the resources of their public office for the betterment of the community of faith.

Old Testament eschatology relativizes the present ruling powers, granting them only provisional validity. Nevertheless, since the powers are ultimately subjected to God's divine rule, it indirectly promotes the work of God in sustaining life in a broken and fallen world. Therefore, the Covenant community cannot retreat into a ghetto given her responsibility to contribute her share in the promotion of relative peace and justice.

The vision of Isaiah 60 strongly prophesied the eventual reclamation of the riches of the nations. This engenders a positive assessment and reception of the gifts of God which bring enrichment to society and culture. Richard Mouw writes of how this vision emphasizes the final inclusion of all races into the Covenant community.[7] The universalism of Isaiah renders unacceptable any narrow ethnocentrism that is so prevalent today. It must be stressed too that the vision of the restored Covenant community rejects any suggestion of dominance or imperialism in any form. Rather the Covenant community must seek to embody the liberating laws of God. By its just laws others will know that her God is the only true God. Good news was to be shared with the afflicted captives and broken hearted (Isa. 61:11–4).

Reconciled Community in Christ

The prophetic expectation was fulfilled through the work of Christ. Specifically, the work of Christ was seen as having broken the dividing wall of hostility (Eph. 2:16) and as establishing a new community. Paul's relational concern is aptly captured by Robert Banks who writes, that

> based on the common experience of reconciliation between the individual and God and the individual and his fellow-men this means "that the focal point of reference was neither a book or a rite *but a set of relationships*, and that God communicated himself to them not primarily through the written word and tradition, or mystical experience and cultic activity but *through one another*.[8]

Because of the inclusive reconciling work of Christ, relationships in the community should transcend all social and ethnic barriers (Gal. 3:28). This injunction does not imply the abolition of legal and social structures as subsuming their functions towards the building of a Covenant (agape) community. That is to say, Paul in contrast to the enthusiasts did not advocate a total rejection of existing social institutions. Allen Verhey explains, "In the 'not yet' character of our existence, equality of slave and free does not create a whole new set of social standards and role assignments. Neither Paul nor the enthusiasts can snap their fingers and produce a whole new social system. But the new age . . . requires new relationships in the midst of old roles."[9]

Commitment towards the Covenant community does not entail rejection of the believers' social status for whatever station they are in. The Christian will conscientiously explore new and creative ways to serve Christ and the neighbor. Cultural forms and social roles are relative. The Christian is free to accept them as provisionally valid provided they are subject to the law of the love and freedom in Christ. The Covenant community allows diversity of cultural roles and celebrates pluralism.

It should be stressed that the Covenant community exists not only to cater to the needs of the well-off and socially adjusted. The remarkable role of the Covenant community lies precisely in its ability to attract and integrate the socially marginalized groups and the underprivileged of society. The message of hope in the Gospel motivates believers to release suppressed energy and redirect it constructively towards building a common community. Marginalization should not generate social apathy. Believers are to strengthen their communal identity and through their caring relationships testify to an alternative and more attractive society. In a sense we may view the Covenant community as a special social experiment to practice a set of values different from those of the larger society. Still, such commitment should not be used as an excuse for social disengagement.

Integrated Household

The Covenant community however should not be merely an impersonal instrument of an abstract social ideology. It is on the contrary seen as a household. The image of a household stirs up feelings of belonging and group identity. It speaks of a faith that addresses the immediate and practical experiences of life. John Elliott stresses the psychological relevance of the Covenant community as the household of God in a society plagued by individual and social alienation. "Here alone were the marginals of society moved to the centre of the world's stage. In this family alone did former outcasts become the elect and privileged people of God. Here alone was a community shaped and motivated by fraternal love, mutual respect and humble service."[10]

It is because Christian duties are seen as responsibility in mutual relationships that it can avoid the dangers of legalism that plague religion. However within the Christian household, duties are not so much requirements of rules and regulations as duties of mutual love. The household satisfies social-psychological needs of making people feel at home in an impersonal world. Of course, Stoicism as a philosophy claimed to provide it, but Christianity brings it down to simple people.

Robert Nisbett suggests that the fundamental struggle between Christianity and the Roman Empire arose from their different conceptions of the family, the meaning of religious community and the values of kinship.[11] Christianity was ascendant for three reasons. Firstly, Christianity was not merely concerned with abstract beliefs. It provided a way of life where members often lived together sharing resources in looking after the welfare of one another. Secondly, Roman society was disintegrating. But Christianity provided a place of refuge, security and order. Thirdly, Christianity successfully adapted a revered social model, the family organized on the basis of *patria potestas*. The Christian central emphasis on the household did not so much reject the concept of kinship as displace it with a deeper kinship in Christ. The Christian household was proffered as the highest of all types of family. Elliott concluded,

> Christianity's response to society is given an integrated accentuation. In its message the strangers, the rootless, the homeless of any age can take comfort: in the community of the faithful the stranger is no longer an isolated alien but a brother or sister. For the *paroikoi* of society there is a possibility of life and communion in the *oikos tou theou*, a home for the homeless.[12]

In summary, the Christian accepts the relative validity of contemporary earthly institutions as the arena whereby he or she discharges faithfully the divine vocation to be a responsible and caring citizen. The community of faith exists to nurture such responsible faith and promotes such ideals that declare God's agenda of transformation of social and cultural life. We end with the fitting advice of Richard Mouw.

> We are called to *await* the coming transformation. But we should await actively, not passively. We must *seek* the City which is to come. Many activities are proper to this "seeking" life. We can call human institutions to obedience to the Creator. . . . And in a special and profound way, we prepare for life in the City when we work actively to bring about healing and obedience in within the community of the people of God.[13]

II. COVENANT AND DEMOCRATIC CONSENSUS IN PLURALISTIC SOCIETY

How can the covenant principle be extended to a broader society that is pluralistic in nature? In this regard, a covenant way of life demands participation in building democratic consensus in modern democratic societies. That is to say, the challenge of any covenant religious community is to nurture citizens who are able to transcend their religious and ethical framework and adopt what Hannah Arendt calls 'enlarged mentality' or 'representative thinking'. Seyla Benhabib describes this as "the capacity to represent to oneself the multiplicity of viewpoints, the variety of perspectives, the layers of meaning which constitute a situation." In other words, good and acceptable moral judgments arise from an exercise of reversibility of perspective either by actually listening to all involved or by representing to ourselves imaginatively the many perspectives of those involved.[14]

It is granted that participants in public deliberation working out democratic consensus operate with different conceptions on what constitutes a sufficient context for dialog. In this regard, Benhabib offers some valuable insights on different conceptions of dialog (or public space). She begins with Hannah Arendt who notes that the public space becomes agonistic when participants in a morally homogeneous and politically egalitarian society compete for recognition, precedence and acclaim. In contrast, an associational public space emerges whenever "men act together in concert" whether as pressure groups in a democracy or as dissidents under a tyranny. Constructive collective action arises when men of good will converse together in the associational public space. However, Arendt has been criticized by Liberals like Bruce Ackerman and John Rawls for failing to be attentive to the institutional preconditions that must be fulfilled for genuine dialog to take place. Such a recognition will make evident and address the connection between power and legitimacy by proposing a procedural solution. Rawls argues,

> Just as a political conception of justice needs certain principles of justice for the basic structure to specify its content, it also needs certain guidelines of enquiry and publicly recognized rules of assessing evidence to govern its application. Otherwise there is no agreed way of determining whether these principles are satisfied, and for settling what they require of particular institutions, or in particular situations. . . .[15]

One recourse is to work towards thin and overlapping consensus. This is typified in many communiques and media statements which follow conferences that have attracted media attention. Such thin consensus are not without value, insofar as they encourage further dialog and possibly call for more inclusive social policies.

It is unfortunate that the Liberal procedural solution envisages a post-life of 'conversational restraint' where participants in the interest of neutrality avoid raising concrete differences. They should each seek to identity normative premises that all political participants find reasonable. But does this requirement not amount to an amputation of political deliberation from the other dimensions of social life from which political action draws its significance, such as life in voluntary associations? Benjamin Barber remarked that the move appears to be "an antipathy to democracy and its sustaining institutional structures (participation, civic education, political activism) and a 'thin' rather than strong version of political life in which citizens are spectators and clients while politicians are professionals who do the actual governing."

Seyla Benhabib argues that the liberal principle of dialogic neutrality "is too restrictive and frozen in application to the dynamics of power struggles in actual political processes. A public life, conducted according to the principle of liberal dialogic neutrality, would not only lack agonistic dimensions of politics, in Arendtian terms, but more severely, it would restrict the scope of public conversion in ways that would be inimical to the interests of oppressed groups . . . liberalism ignores the "agonistic" dimension of public-political life"[16] As such, dialog must highlight the inherent difference that we must accept and incorporate into social policies.

A more critical and inclusive model of public space and dialogue is found in Jurgen Habermas' proposal of ideal speech situation and discourse ethics. Habermas suggests, "The goal of coming to an understanding is to bring about an agreement that terminates in the intersubjective mutuality of reciprocal understanding, shared knowledge, mutual trust, and accord with one another. Agreement is based on recognition of the corresponding validity claims of comprehensibility, truthfulness, and rightness."[17]

Habermas' ideals demand that participants come in good faith and lay out clearly the grounds of their assertions, backed with rational argumentation with the expectation that the validity of these claims will be tested critically. Habermas insists that views that prevail under such conditions are those that are more rational—arguing, persuading and winning consent without coercion. By the same token, views that prevail exemplify and promote positive social conditions such as genuineness, integrity, fairness, equality and democratic consensus. These outcomes are more than pragmatic expedience since they flow from rational consensus with its immanent normativity. Habermas, however, rejects that these norms become normative because they spring from an overarching metaphysical framework. Instead, they prevail if they create free space while promoting the good life of individuals through democratic means.

Habermas adopts a cognitive approach, confident that moral problems can be solved through rational and cognitive means. He is confident that norms derived from his discourse ethics will be accepted since the discourse merely universalizes moral principles embedded in dialog situations and is impartial in its implementation. In other words, a norm is valid only if "all affected can accept the consequences and the side effects . . . (and these consequences are preferred to those of known alternative possibilities)."[18]

Notwithstanding the rigor of Habermas' analysis, I cannot help but feel that his confident expectation of moral agreement through a universalized rationality and his ideal speech situation have an unreality about them if we bear in mind the interminable disagreements among the best minds in academia. Further weaknesses become clear. First, focusing on universal rationality leads to insufficient attention given to the role power plays in dialog especially in dialogic situations which bring together partners with unequal resources. It is only too easy for the assertive participants to overwhelm the weaker ones under the guise of more winsome articulation, or for the majority to impose their views on others.

Nevertheless, Habermas' requirements serves as an effective regulative ideal which effectively unmasks majoritians who are more interested in manipulation rather than dialog. Benhabib builds on these Habermasian ideals by formalizing a procedure of "historically self-conscious universalism" which among others include a set of procedural rules that reflect the moral ideal that "we ought to *respect* each other as beings whose standpoint is worthy of equal consideration (the principle of universal moral respect)" and that "we ought to treat each other as concrete beings whose capacity to express this standpoint we ought to enhance by creating, wherever possible, social practices embodying the discursive ideal (the principle of egalitarian reciprocity)."[19]

Second, the dialogic selves envisaged by Habermas lose their moral concreteness given his focus on abstract criteria and rarefied universal rationality leading to a neglect of the positive resources embodied in the moral traditions of participants. In fact, we doubt if there are unencumbered selves with universal rationality. As Mary Midgley once quipped, no one speaks universal languages. In contrast, dialogue promises depth and fruitfulness only if participants are able to bring maximum input in the first place. Therein lies the dilemma: inclusion of moral diversity enriches the dialogue. But this also increases the likelihood of irresolvable conflict. Perhaps Habermasian dialog seeks to avoid such conflicts as it only serves to confirm the essentially contestable nature of concepts like good life, justice and diverse primary goods of democracy.[20]

On the other hand, acknowledgement of the essentially contestable nature of dialogic issues will encourage a more tempered acceptance of pluralism which need not be subsumed under some universal criteria or rationality. Still dialog must address the issue of pluralism without succumbing to relativism. After all, is it not the fear of relativism that leads some participants to resort to power manipulation? The insights of Alasdair McIntyre and Charles Taylor on evaluating traditional bound rationality offer some promising alternatives to coercive universal rationality on the one hand and sentimental and subversive relativism on the other.

McIntyre agrees that we cannot appeal to 'neutral' criteria to adjudicate between competing traditions. Nor should we compare rival positions against independent facts so much as to lay out how the new conclusion must be accepted on premises that both sides accept. As Taylor explains MacIntyre's position, "What may convince us that a given transition from X to Y is a gain is not only or even so much how X and Y deal with the facts, but how they deal with one another. . . . In adopting Y, we make better sense not just of the world, but of our history of trying to explain the world, part of which has been played out in terms of X."[21]

Taylor modestly suggests that the claim is not that Y is absolutely true, but that whatever is 'ultimately true,' "Y is better than X. It is, one might say, less false . . . whatever else turns out to be true, you can improve your epistemic position by moving from X to Y; this is a gain."[22] Taylor emphasizes that such a move does not amount to a claim to have arrived at the final rational explanation. It is rather a choice for the best explanation so far. More important than merely being more rational is a concomitant requirement to be morally responsible for our epistemological choices.

Being tradition bound, we acknowledge then that moral discernment and responsibility never occur *ex nihilo*. Our choices and ethical justification are inherently the outcome of the moral resources that we draw from our religious and cultural tradition. We must therefore address the reality that there are different ethical traditions in our pluralistic society. That being the case, the challenge then is for each religion in a pluralistic society to demonstrate that it has the resources necessary to build an inclusive society that is just and moral.

Covenant Politics in Society

The Christian tradition has historically favored the following criteria for ethical valuation of competing moral choices. Any ethics will have to display: (1) Power to release us from destructive alternatives; (2) Ways of seeing through current distortions; (3) Room to keep us from having to resort to violence; (4) A sense for the tragic—how meaning transcends power.[23] It should be noted that the criteria recognize the dark side of human moral existence that is not addressed by proponents for universal rationality. The criteria are not meant to be applied mechanically for the sole purpose of rational valuation. Instead the very adoption of these criteria must be seen as a commitment to a way of life, a determined effort to embody the moral vision in a community.

Such an outlook suggests that bringing one's religion into the project of building a shared society does not necessarily result in dominance and coercion. It is granted that some people hesitate to bring in religion because religion has be en exploited to legitimize unjust social orders. However, religion per se is neither intrinsically conservative or revolutionary. Religion is only part of a complex of social factors, which usually includes race and economics, leading to any exploitation and conflict. On the other hand it can be argued that a healthy polity is dependent on values sustained by religion. The challenge is to find an appropriate placing of religion in society in a social covenant, a democratic constitution. The following proposals should be worthy of consideration:

1. Religions must renounce abuse of power.

I think the appropriate response from all religions is to reject publicly any abuse of religion for political gains and to avail their ethical resources for the building of a consensus that makes common life possible in a multi-religious society. We welcome the humility of religious leaders reported in the "Declaration of a Global Ethic" from the Parliament of World Religions in Chicago. The Declaration says, "Time and again we see leaders and members of religions incite aggression, fanaticism, hate and xenophobia —even inspire and legitimize violent and bloody conflicts. . . . We are filled with disgust." The Parliament further recommended four ethical imperatives: (1) A culture of non- violence and reverence for all life, (2) A culture of social solidarity with a just economic system, (3) A culture of tolerance and honesty and (4) a culture of equal treatment for, and partnership between, men and women.

2. Religions must offer their ethical resources vital for building consensus and harmony in society.

The studies of Robert Bellah and his team of researchers highlight that the problem of contemporary society is not merely the precariousness of the bonds of citizenship but a more fundamental problem of people's inability to bond and build relationships.[24] Obviously such bonding needs to be stimulated by primal patterns of association exemplified by religion. Religious social functions need to go beyond individual therapy (self-actualization, fulfillment) and contribute directly to the common life of society.

It is precisely when individual needs are adequately met that religion is put forward as a foundational tool for social projects. That is to say, religion contributes its best in the life of robust moral individuals. These individuals will in turn bring morality into the public square and the market place without harboring an illusion of religious aggrandizement by religious clerics who see themselves as harbingers of social progress. The apt phrase coined by Reinhold Niebuhr, "Moral Men in Immoral Society," succinctly captures the positive function of religion. Religion then promotes healthy national life by ensuring that it is underpinned by "communities of character."

Democracy has emerged as the unchallenged political ideal in the Third World. But democracy requires disciplined citizens in order to function properly. John Wogaman explains,

> A democratic society is well served by a citizenry not fanatically attached to single issues or causes but capable of rounded judgment and a careful weighing of ambiguous alternatives. That maturity is grounded, first, in a secure sense of personal worth. And it is at this point that the personal faith of Christians is a distinct contribution to democratic disciplines.[25]

It is vital that each religion spells out how its beliefs specifically contribute to the building of a common society where human dignity is respected and where the only force accepted is the force of truth in a fair and equal dialogue. The purpose is to set up a social and political mechanism that promotes virtue and compromise. Public democracy is sustained by private virtues that enable individuals to set aside personal interests. A sense of transcendent authority typified by the Christian God of grace will encourage politics to be conducted by rules of courtesy, mutual respect, fair dealings and personal integrity that cross communities. With such democratic disciplines potential conflicts are more likely to be resolved and demagogues will find it more difficult to exploit 'primordial sentiments' for their personal gain.

3. We need a public philosophy that allows for diversity in unity.

Social conflicts arise when different communities fail to practice tolerance and mutual acceptance that recognizes differences. All too often national integration is implemented on terms set *by* the dominant community because it is assumed that unity requires homogeneity. Should we not instead accept plurality within unity as a given reality in the contemporary world even though we want to place plurality within a wider framework *of* transcendent values? Speaking on behalf *of* Christianity (and I shall assume that such a defense is also a possibility for other religions) I want to suggest that democratic pluralism is a practical consequence *of* the Christian doctrine *of* Trinity. Max Stackhouse offers a pertinent Trinitarian grounding for democratic pluralism.

For those of us who believe that the Trinitarian God is the true God, pluralism is a normative theological belief as well as an ethical or social belief. The metaphysical, moral grounds for dealing with pluralism are at hand. Pluralism within a dynamic unity, understood in terms of persons in community and the community of persons, . . . it gives metaphysical-moral articulation to the proper foundations and limits of pluralism. Christians oppose monolithic definition of ultimate reality, but their pluralistic beliefs are governed by a broader belief in unity. The triune God is integrated. Thus polytheism, the theological form of pluralism without unity, is condemned as strongly as is imperious singleness without differentiation. In using these terms, we see that both pluralism and unity can become blessings or curses, depending on whether our view of pluralism has an ultimate coherence, or whether our view of unity has a place for diversity.[26]

In conclusion we should recognize that each one of us enters the public sphere as a person shaped by prior commitments that are pre-political. The public sphere is a place for dialogue, bargaining and compromises. Compromises as such should not be seen as objectionable, or a reflection of moral timidity. It is a responsible act necessary for fallen people to live peacefully with one another, without which democracy will be replaced by the law of the jungle.

NOTES

1. Ray Anderson, *Historical Transcendence and the Reality of God* (Grand Rapids, MI: Eerdmans, 1975), p.82.

2. Vincent Brummer, *Theological & Philosophical Inquiry* (London: MacMillan, 1981), chapter 2.

3. Jerry H. Gill, *The Possibility of Religious Knowledge* (Grand Rapids, MI: Eerdmans, 1971), p.115.

4. Paul Hanson, *The People Called: The Growth of Community in the Bible* (New York: Harper and Row, 1986), p. 470.

5. Walter Bruggemann, *Interpretation and Obedience* (Minneapolis, MN: Fortress, 1991), pp. 148, 151.

6. Christopher Wright, *An Eye For an Eye* (Downers Grove, IL: IVP, 1983), p. 101.

7. See Richard Mouw's book, *When the Kings Come Marching In: Isaiah and the New Jerusalem* (Grand Rapids, MI: Eerdmans, 1983).

8. Robert Banks, *Paul's Idea of Community* (Grand Rapids, MI: Eerdmans, 1980), p. 111.

9. Allen Verhey, *The Great Reversal* (Grand Rapids, MI: Eerdmans, 1984), p. 114.

10. John Elliott, *A Home for the Homeless* (Minneapolis, MN: Fortress, 1981), p. 231.

11. R.A. Nisbet, *The Social Philosophers: Community and Conflict in Western Thought* (Victoria, BC: Thomas Cromwell, 1973), pp. 174–181.

12. Elliott, pp. 266–268.

13. Richard Mouw, *When the Kings Come Marching In* (Grand Rapids, MI: Eerdmans, 1983), p. 75.

14. Seyla Benhabib, *Situating the Self* (New York: Routledge, 1992), pp. 53–54.

15. Quoted in Benhabib, p. 101.

16. Quoted in Benhabib, p. 100.

17. Habermas, "What is Universal Pragmatics?" in Jurgen Habermas, *Communication and the Evolution of Society* (Heinemann, 1975).

18. Jurgen Habermas, *Discourse Ethics: Notes on a Program of Philosophical Justification* (Cambridge, MA: MIT Press, 1990), p. 65.

19. Benbabib, p. 31.

20. For an approach that acknowledges the irreducible diversity of social goods, see Michael Walzer, *Spheres of Justice* (New York: Basic Books, 1983).

21. Charles Taylor, *Philosophical Arguments* (Cambridge, MA: Harvard University Press, 1995), p. 43.

22. Ibid., p. 54.

23. Stanley Hauerwas, "From System to Story: An Alternative Pattern for Rationality in Ethics" co-written with David B. Burrell in Stanley Hauerwas, *Truthfulness and Tragedy* (Notre Dame, IN: University of Notre Dame Press, 1977), p.35.

24. Robert Bellah et. al., *Habits of the Heart* (New York: Harper & Row, 1985), p.137.

25. John P. Wogaman, *Christian Perspectives on Politics* (London: SCM, 1988), p.175.

26. Max Stackhouse, *Public Theology and Political Economy* (Grand Rapids, MI: Eerdmans, 1987), p. 163.

Chapter Five

THE ISHMAEL PROMISES: A BRIDGE FOR MUTUAL RESPECT

Jonathan Edwin Culver
Professor of Theology
Tyranus Biblical Seminary
Bandung, Indonesia

The destruction of the Manhattan World Trade Center on September 11, 2001, has been indelibly etched into our collective memories. Who can forget the incredible images of the collapsing twin towers, imploding with a deafening roar? Three thousand souls perished in that one horrific moment, mostly office workers from the United States and other western nations. Several hundred workers from Asian and Muslim majority nations were also numbered among the victims, including nationals from Turkey. September 11 was an act of terror perpetrated by fanatics from Arab/Muslim backgrounds. Yet, for the sake of balance, we should also recall examples of Christian terrorism, the most recent being the slaughter of innocent Bosnian and Kosovar Muslims by fanatic Serbian Christians. We should not allow the al-Qaeda terrorism of September 11 to eclipse the less dramatic but equally demonic Serbian terrorism of the 1990's.

Do these two examples of recent extremist terrorism indicate that Islam and Christianity are on an inevitable collision course leading to a final "clash of civilizations?" There are some who seem to think so,[1] and terrorist groups from both religions fervently hope for such a scenario. A civilizational clash may be a possibility, but it is not inevitable. I say this from my perspective as a Christian theology professor who has lived for 20 years in the world's largest Muslim nation, Indonesia. The vast majority of Muslims and Christians in Indonesia (or elsewhere for that matter) abhor the concept of a civilizational clash. More importantly, it appears that followers of the world's two largest religions are even willing to take significant steps, separately and together, to prevent such a catastrophe from happening. One step in the direction towards peace are the papers in this volume.

PURPOSE AND SCOPE OF THIS STUDY

In an effort to build bridges of respect between Muslims and Christians I have chosen to highlight God's promises to Abraham and Hagar regarding their son Ishmael in the biblical account of Genesis (in the *Tawrat*). I have decided upon this approach in response to an excellent article by Riffat Hassan which she presented at another Muslim-Christian dialogue in 1994. In her article entitled, "Eid al-Adha (Feast of Sacrifice) in Islam: Abraham, Hagar and Ishmael," Riffat, a devout Muslim scholar, invited those from other religions to consider deeply the significance of Abraham, Hagar, and Ishmael as commemorated by Islam's ritual of sacrifice.[2] In her paper, Hassan quoted extensively from an Islamic religious text, the Hadith of al-Bukhari.[3] One important reason why I appreciated Hassan's paper was because al-Bukhari's account of the Abraham, Hagar and Ishmael story resembled the one in my own religious text in Genesis. Here was a bridge for me, as a Christian, to appreciate and understand a Muslim perspective. I sensed that Hassan was inviting me to walk out on this bridge to a meeting point of common ideas in the middle.

What I would like to do now is extend to Muslim readers an invitation to make the same kind of journey that I made with Hassan. To do this I want to give an opportunity for Muslims to reflect on a religious text outside of their tradition, just as Hassan invited me to consider a text from her tradition. Between Genesis chapter 16 and 21 we find stirring accounts in which God or His angel speaks directly to Abraham and Hagar. In these passages God gives four remarkable promises concerning Ishmael. Furthermore, on two occasions God intervenes dramatically to save the life of Hagar and her son. The Genesis narratives also recount how God established the lad Ishmael in the wilderness in order that he might fulfill his destiny. Many of these same themes are also found in Islam where Ishmael emerges as a central figure along with his father Abraham.[4]

A reflection on the Hagar-Ishmael narratives in Genesis would also be useful to Christian readers. Because of the history of wars and polemics between the Christian and Muslim religious communities, Christians throughout the ages have tended to overlook or distort the Hagar-Ishmael story in their own Scriptures.[5] Thus both Muslim and Christian believers would profit by reading this text; Muslims could read a Judaeo-Christian text that honors Hagar and Ishmael, and Christians could see God's compassion and providential care for two figures whom Muslims highly esteem. This is not to say, however, that the two faith communities will always agree on the specific details in the Genesis account. Yet, if we can look beyond these disagreements and refrain from crude attempts at forcing our distinct perspectives, or theological persuasions upon one another, then we might discover important bridges of communication in key theological areas.[6] This would provide a foundation to enable the two sides to mutually esteem one another.

A question that might arise here is, why should Muslims be asked to read the *Tawrat* when they already have such a rich tradition relative to Hagar and Ishmael? At this point it is helpful to realize that for more than a thousand years Muslims have read these accounts in Genesis and found blessing in them.[7] One Muslim who gave an extensive commentary on the Genesis text is 'Ali ibn Rabbin Tabari (early third century A.H./late ninth century A.D.). From a Christian standpoint, his exegesis on Hagar and Ishmael is, for the most part, quite fair and refreshing. It is found in his work, the *Kitab al-Din wa'l-Dawla* (*The Book of Religion and Empire*).[8] He wrote this work to remove the doubts and skepticism toward the divine origins of Islam on the part of non-Muslims, especially Christians, whom Tabari addresses as "my cousins." He was conversant with the Judaeo-Christian scriptures, and furthermore, he did not deny the integrity of the biblical text.[9] As a result, Harry G. Dorman describes the work as "a serious and not unfriendly approach" rather than "a polemic of bitterness and abuse" towards Christianity.[10]

THREE KEY ISHMAEL PASSAGES FROM GENESIS

If my readers can accept the invitation to reflect with me on the Ishmael narratives in Genesis, I will begin by explaining my approach. The texts that I have chosen are Genesis 16:7–13, 17:18–21, and 21:9–21. After I provide some needed information on the context and background, I will then quote an English translation of these texts from the *New Revised Standard Version* of the Bible. Next, I will make personal theological comments on them but give exegetical explanations and contextual commentary in the footnotes. These reflections on the texts summarize some of the key ideas in my dissertation on the Ishmael promises in Genesis. They also draw from a book that I wrote for the Christians of Indonesia.[11] I also wish to state here that personal reflection on these texts has given me a deeper appreciation for Muslims.

GENESIS 16:7–13: AN ACT OF DIVINE REDEMPTION

Genesis 16:7–13, relates the account of Hagar, who flees from the wrath and oppression of Sarah, Abraham's first wife. Earlier, in 16:4–6 Sarah punishes Hagar for exhibiting pride after becoming pregnant, while she herself suffers the humiliation of barrenness (Gen. 16:4).[12] As a result Hagar flees, and takes the wilderness road leading to Shur, on the border of Egypt. Hagar the Egyptian (Gen. 16:1) is apparently running home to her family. But this is a dangerous road for a single woman pregnant with child. God, however, in His mercy sends the "angel of the Lord" to talk with her while she is resting by a well. There he persuades her to return to Abraham's tent. To encourage her to overcome her fear and obey God's command, the angel gives Hagar a marvelous promise:

> The angel of the Lord found her by a spring of water in the wilderness, the spring on the way to Shur. And he said, "Hagar, slave-girl of Sarai, where have you come from and where are you going?" She said, "I am running away from my mistress Sarai." The angel of the Lord said to her, "Return to your mistress, and submit to her." The angel of the Lord also said to her, "I will so greatly multiply your descendants that they cannot be counted for multitude." And the angel of the Lord said to her, "Now you have conceived and shall bear a son; you shall call him Ishmael,[13] for the Lord has given heed to your affliction. He shall be a wild ass of a man,[14] with his hand against everyone, and everyone's hand against him; and he shall be at odds with all his kin."[15] So she named the Lord who spoke to her, "You are El-roi,"[16] for she said, "Have I really seen God and remained alive after seeing him?" (Gen.16:7–13).

Genesis 16:7–13 is a story of God's great mercy for the oppressed. Therefore it is fitting to emphasize the God-centered aspects of this text. For Christians, God's action on behalf of Hagar falls in the category of his redemptive and saving acts. Hagar was a victim of Sarah's wrath, but according to Genesis 16:4 she was not entirely blameless. And yet God is very merciful to her. This signifies God's grace with the intention that change will result based on gratitude. Thus the angel of the Lord intervenes to deliver Hagar and her unborn child from possible harm in the desert. In the process he dignifies her with a promise of descendants "too many to count" (16:10). The wording here is reminiscent of the Abrahamic covenant promise of Genesis 15:5.[17] God offers Hagar a destiny as the progenitress of one branch among Abraham's offspring—if she obeys the angel's command to return to Abraham's tent. Apparently, God has some unfinished business relating to all of Abraham's family—Sarah, Hagar and Ishmael included. Among other things we could conclude that God wished to place Ishmael under the care of his righteous father.

Although the promise of 16:10–12 is made to Hagar, its fulfillment will come through Ishmael (cf., Gen. 17:20; 21:13, 19). Therefore, we can rightfully call it an "Ishmaelite promise." The redemptive connotation in the promise is striking. While Ishmael is still in the womb God blesses him with a name that conveys a promise. In Hebrew, *yishma'e'l* means "God hears" or,

"God will hear." We encounter two other instances of word play on this name in Genesis 17:20 and 21:17: "As for Ishmael, I have heard you" and "God heard the voice of the boy." The fact that God's hearing relates to Hagar's affliction is a key component in the promissory aspect in Ishmael's name. The text says, "you shall call him Ishmael, for the Lord has given heed [literally "heard"] to your affliction." Thus Hagar's affliction is commemorated in the name of her son and among those called "Ishmaelites." Her story indicates that God is a God of justice and delivers the afflicted when they call on his name.

GENESIS 17:18–21:
THE IMPLICATIONS FOR MUSLIM ORIGINS

The next passage recounts an event that took place thirteen years after the birth of Ishmael in Genesis 16 (cf. Gen. 16:16 with 17:1). For background, we need to start with 17:3–6, where God Almighty (Hebrew, *el-shaddai*) promises Abraham many descendants and future greatness (17:3–6), and commands him to circumcise himself and all the males in his household, including Ishmael (17:10–11, 23–27). However, God startles Abraham with the announcement that Sarah will bear him a son in his old age. At this point, Abraham remembers Ishmael. With great concern he prays to God, saying, "O that Ishmael might live in your sight!" (Gen. 17:18). In reply, God gives Abraham a qualified answer. His answer includes both a "no" component and a "yes" component. God's answer in 17:19 is "no" if Abraham is asking that Ishmael replace Isaac as the son whom God chooses to uphold his covenant. To emphasize this point God states the matter twice in 17:19 and in 17:21.[18] Abu'l-Fath al-Shahrastini (d.1153 A. D.) provides an Islamic perspective on this matter of God's choice of the Isaac-Jacob line in *al-Milal wa'n-Nihal* or, *Religious Communities and Creeds*.[19] Shahrastini explains that the line of Isaac was the scripture-bearing line of the prophetic heritage from Abraham to Jesus, whereas the line of Ishmael was essentially a "silent line" entrusted with the custody of God's House in Mecca along with its rituals. With the advent of Muhammad, however, the line of Isaac receded in importance and then both lines were joined together under the aegis of the Final Prophet. This statement by Shahrastini, however, does not square with Genesis 17:19, where God says that he would establish his covenant with Isaac "forever". I see this as one of those unbridgeable theological statements where Christians and Muslims must agree to disagree. Hopefully, we can continue to respect each other even if we do not see eye-to-eye. Putting disagreements aside for now, we do see that in 17:20 God states that he is willing to bless Ishmael.

And Abraham said to God, "O that Ishmael might live in your sight!" God said, "No, but your wife Sarah shall bear you a son, and you shall name him Isaac. I will establish my covenant with him as an everlasting covenant for his offspring after him. As for Ishmael, I have heard you; I will bless him and make him fruitful[20] and exceedingly numerous; he shall be the father of twelve princes, and I will make him a great nation. But my covenant I will establish with Isaac, whom Sarah shall bear to you at this season next year (Gen. 17:18–21).

As we continue to focus upon the divine perspective I would like to argue that the promises for Ishmael in Genesis 17 provide a Christian theological foundation to answer an important question. Is there a divine cause for the rise of more than one billion people on planet earth who call themselves "Muslims?"[21] The data from the Ishmael promise in Genesis 17:20 reveals some significant points to consider in answering this question. We need to recall that the promise to Ishmael as the imprimatur of a divine guarantee as witnessed by the words, "I will make him fruitful" and "cause him to multiply."[22] In contrast, Adam and Noah were merely commanded to be fruitful and populate the earth (Gen. 1:28; 8:17; 9:1, 7). Here in 17:20 the verbal forms suggest that God will guarantee Ishmael's success in accomplishing this task. The force of this promise surely goes beyond the confines of a single generation, namely, Ishmael's twelve sons as listed in the genealogy of Genesis 25:12–18.

Secondly, we need to see how the promises and blessings for Ishmael have kept pace with those given to Abraham. In 17:6 Abraham receives a covenant, which includes fruitfulness, nations, and kings.[23] In Genesis 17:20 Ishmael is granted a promise of blessing, which includes fruitfulness, princes, and a nation. For Ishmael this blessing in 17:20 is considerably better than the first promise of 16:10–12. The degree of improvement has kept pace with the improvement in the promise made to Abraham in Genesis 17, which significantly raises the level of the first Abrahamic promise in Genesis 12:1–3. This suggests that Ishmael's promises are dynamically related to the covenant oaths that God extends to Abraham. Indeed, many of the components of the Abrahamic blessing also appear in the blessing for Ishmael (with the exception of the distinctive covenant promise, "in you all peoples will find blessing"). This affinity with the broader components of the Abrahamic covenant endows the promise for Ishmael with dignity, blessing and lasting impact upon the latter and his descendants. Therefore, God's promise in Genesis 17:20 may very well be the foundational principle that has given rise to more than a billion Muslims today, the majority of whom live outside the Middle East.[24]

GENESIS 21:9–21: A CASE FOR DIVINE PROVIDENCE

This final passage describes the sending away of Hagar and Ishmael by Abraham on account of pressure from Sarah. Perhaps Sarah feels that when Ishmael grows up he will become a threat to Isaac and take his inheritance (cf. 21:10). Abraham opposes Sarah's request, and had God not intervened the patriarchal pair might have experienced a rupture in their relations. Although for some readers it might seem odd that God would support Sarah over against Abraham, we should note that God does promise to make Ishmael a great nation. Abraham understands from this that God will protect Hagar and Ishmael in the wilderness. Thus he finds some solace in this even though God places upon him a very difficult task. Thus God preserves unity in Abraham's household and at the same time uses this incident to display his providential care. From 21:14 onward, Muslim readers will find broad parallels to the Abraham-Hagar-Ishmael story of Ibn 'Abbas as told in the Hadith of al-Bukhari.[25]

> But Sarah saw the son of Hagar the Egyptian, whom she had borne to Abraham, playing with her son Isaac. So she said to Abraham, "Cast out this slave woman and her son; for the son of this slave woman shall not inherit along with my son Isaac." The matter was very distressing to Abraham on account of his son.[26] But God said to Abraham, "Do not be distressed because of the boy and because of your slave woman; whatever Sarah says to you, do as she tells you,[27] for it is through Isaac that offspring shall be named[28] after you. As for the son of the slave woman, I will make a nation of him also, because he is your offspring."[29] So Abraham rose early in the morning, and took bread and a skin of water, and gave it to Hagar, putting it on her shoulder, along with the child,[30] and sent her away. And she departed, and wandered about in the wilderness of Beer-sheba. When the water in the skin was gone, she cast[31] the child under one of the bushes. Then she went and sat down opposite him a good way off, about the distance of a bowshot; for she said, "Do not let me look on the death of the child." And as she sat opposite him, she lifted up her voice and wept. And God heard[32] the voice of the boy; and the angel of God called to Hagar from heaven, and said to her, "What troubles you, Hagar? Do not be afraid; for God has heard the voice of the boy where he is. Come, lift up the boy and hold him fast with your hand, for I will make a great nation of him." Then God opened her eyes, and she saw a well of water. She went, and filled the skin with water, and gave the boy a drink. God was with the boy, and he grew up; he lived in the wilderness, and became an expert with the bow. He lived in the wilderness of Paran;[33] and his mother got a wife for him from the land of Egypt (Gen. 21:9–21).

If Genesis 17 contains God's promise to make Ishmael into a great nation, Genesis 21 sets the stage for that promise to take effect. At this point in the story Hagar and Ishmael must leave Abraham's house. Sarah has demanded it, and the text reports that God himself commands Abraham to comply with Sarah's wishes. Whatever may be God's reasons, Abraham is certain of this one fact: God will provide for Hagar and her son because of the divine promise: "I will make a nation of him [Ishmael] also" (21:13).

In light of Abraham's rejection of Sarah's demands in 21:11, he must have experienced deep emotional anguish when he sent Hagar and Ishmael away. Martin Luther, the father of the Christian Protestant Reformation of the sixteenth century A.D., empathized deeply with Abraham's feelings when he wrote the following commentary on verse 14:

> It is surely a piteous description, which I can hardly read with dry eyes, that the mother and her son bear their expulsion with such patience and go away into exile. Therefore, Father Abraham either stood there with tears in his eyes or followed them with his blessings and prayers as they went away, or he hid himself somewhere in a nook, where he wept in solitude over his own misfortune and that of the exiles.[34]

Then as mother and child go out into the wilderness of Beer-sheba they seem to lose their way. Soon their meager supply of food and water disappears and Ishmael succumbs to heat and exhaustion. Hagar herself has lost all hope. After she lays Ishmael under a bush she goes off to weep, unwilling to see him die. Ishmael also weeps, and it is the sound of Ishmael's voice that moves God to act: "And God heard the voice of the boy" (21:17). God hears, he cares for this lad, and he now moves to save his life. An angel from heaven calls out to Hagar. The fact that the angel spoke from heaven adds to the authority of his words. We also need to hear the compassion and kindness in the angel's voice (remember, he acts and speaks on behalf of God). First he says, "Don't be afraid." Then, he urges Hagar to lift the boy up and hold him fast, for God will make a great nation of him. Then he opens Hagar's eyes to see a well of life-giving water.

The well was there all along but Hagar in her exhausted state could not see it. God had to open her eyes (21:19) before she could avail herself of the water. What a lovely picture of God's immeasurable grace. He speaks comforting words (through the angel) and he performs marvelous deeds on behalf of the needy and the helpless. This is also a marvelous example of the faithfulness of God's promises. He had promised Abraham that Ishmael would become a great nation. For a moment it seemed that the promise would fail. But *El-Shaddai*, God Almighty (Gen. 17:1) is a promise-keeper, the greatest one of all.

The passage ends with a statement that underscores God's providence: "God was with the boy, and he grew up; he lived in the wilderness and became an expert with the bow" (21:20). The meaning of God's presence with

Ishmael here in 21:20, points to the preservation of this boy along with his descendants because verse 21 describes Hagar valiantly shouldering the responsibility of finding a suitable wife for her son. It should be noted here that this was no ordinary providence. Rather, it is akin to the kind of providence that the Christian theologian Louis Berkhof categorizes as "special providence." According to Berkhof, this particular kind of divine grace comes in answer to prayer and deliverance from critical circumstances.[35] Who prayed for Ishmael? We see that Abraham did in Genesis 17:18. Presumably, Abraham continued to pray for him thereafter. Was Ishmael delivered from critical circumstances? He most certainly was. But for what purpose? The Genesis text does not really answer this question with precision. Based on the verses that we have examined it appears that God intervened to save Ishmael's life because of his promise to Abraham. Moreover, the data indicates that even though Isaac and his descendants are entrusted with the unique "covenant promises," Ishmael and his descendants are nevertheless special recipients of God's mission to all nations. The purpose of this divine mission is to bring wholeness and well-being, along with justice and salvation.

CONCLUSION

The invitation by Riffat Hassan for Christians to consider Abraham, Hagar and Ishmael from her perspective as a "Muslim believer" has now come full circle. I have invited Muslim readers to consider these three paradigmatic figures from a Christian perspective which I hope has come across as compassionate and fair. I have also asked Christian readers to take a deeper look at a text which they may have read before, but perhaps had not seen all that God has for Ishmael and his descendants. As the reader can tell, I have written from the standpoint of a "Christian believer" and not simply as a disinterested scholar. Some of those engaged in encounter between the religions would rather confine dialogue to non-theological issues such as justice, peace, and economic and social issues. While these are important, dialogue on the deepest level must also engage faith issues in a spirit of decency and mutual respect. This is a key component in achieving world peace between Muslims and Christians.

NOTES

1. Samuel P. Huntington would not want to say that a clash of civilizations is inevitable, but he nevertheless arranges his evidence and arguments in a manner that

points in that direction. *The Clash of Civilizations and the Remaking of World Order* (London: Touchstone, 1998).

2. Riffat Hassan, "'Eid al-Adha (Feast of Sacrifice) in Islam: Abraham, Hagar and Ishmael." In *Commitment and Commemoration: Jews, Christians, Muslims in Dialogue*. André LaCocque, ed. (Chicago, IL: Exploration, 1994.)

3. For this account readers may wish to consult a parallel Arabic-English version edited and translated by Muhammad Muhsin Khan, *The Translation of the Meanings of Sahih Al-Bukhari* (Beirut, Lebanon: Dar Al-Arabia), Vol 4, pp. 379–382.

4. Muslims regard Abraham and Ishmael as paradigmatic figures on account of their complete submission to the will of God (al-Saffat [37]:100–112). Moreover, according to the ancient Muslim genealogists the Prophet Muhammad is a descendant of Ishmael through his son Qedar (*Qaydar*), or possibly through Nebaioth (*Nabat*) (cf. al-Tabari *Muhammad at Mecca*. W. Montgomery Watt, trans. Vol. 6 of *The History of al-Tabari*. Ehsan Yar-Shater, gen. ed. (Albany, NY: State University of New York Press, 1988). pp. 38–42).

The twelve passages in the Qur'an that mention Ishmael's name are: al-Baqara [2]:125, al-Baqara [2]:127, al-Baqara [2]:133, al-Baqara [2]:136, al-Baqara [2]:140, Al 'Imran [3]:84, al-Nisa [4]:163, al-An'am [6]:86, Ibrahim [14]:39, Maryam [19]:54–55, al-Anbiya' [21]:85, Sad [38]:48. Furthermore, nearly all Muslims today think that Ishmael is the un-named son of Abraham divinely appointed for sacrifice in al-Saffat [37]:100–112.

A very thorough survey and form-critical analysis of Ishmael in the Hadith, Islamic exegesis, and Muslim popular literature is found in Reuben Firestone's *Journeys in Holy Lands: The Evolution of the Abraham-Ishmael Legends in Islamic Exegesis.* (Albany, NY: State University of New York, 1990).

5. For a classic Christian source that gives a negative interpretation of the Ishmael narratives in Genesis see, John Drew Bate, *An Examination of the Claims of Ishmael as Viewed by Muhammadans* (London: Allen and Unwin, 1884). Yet, throughout the centuries some key Christian thinkers have expressed wonder at the ways God spoke and dealt with Hagar and Ishmael. This important community of witness in Christianity has almost been forgotten today. For examples see Culver, "The Ishmael Promises in the Light of God's Mission: Christian and Muslim Reflections" (Ph. D. dissertation, Fuller Theological Seminary, 2001). Also, the chapter on Hagar and her son Ishmael in John L. Thompson, *Writing the Wrongs: Women of the Old Testament among Biblical Commentators from Philo through the Reformation* (New York: Oxford University Press, 2001), pp. 17–99.

6. To see an honest statement of the differences among Christian and Muslim views of Abraham, Hagar and Ishmael, consult Karl-Josef Kushel, *Abraham: Sign of Hope for Jews, Christians, and Muslims* (New York: Continuum, 1995). For a conservative Christian view which differs at many significant point from Muslim perspectives consult my own Ph.D. dissertation, "The Ishmael Promises in the Light of God's Mission: Christian and Muslim Reflections" (Culver, 2001). For another somewhat different approach but similar in spirit to my own, see the doctoral dissertation by a Christian-Arab, Tony Maalouf, "Ishmael in Biblical History" (Ph.D. dissertation, Dallas Theological Seminary, 1998). For a Muslim perspectives on Ishmael see, *Hajj*

by the Iranian author Ali Shariati (Bedford, OH, 1978) and also, the excellent article by Riffat Hassan (1994) that I mentioned above.

7. For example, early Muslim writers like Ibn Qutayba, Ibn al-Djawzi, and al-Mawardi often quoted Bible verses regarding Ishmael, his son Qedar, in their "Proofs or Signs of Prophethood" literature (*Dala'il* or *A'lam al-Nubuwwa*) and in works on other religions and Muslim sects (*Milal wa'l-Nial*). For specific citations and quotes see, Hava Lazarus-Yafeh, *Intertwined Worlds: Medieval Islam and Bible Criticism* (Princeton, NJ: Princeton University Press, 1992), pp. 92–93, 97. Also, Camilla Adang, *Muslim Writers on Judaism and the Hebrew Bible: From Ibn Rabban to Ibn Hazm* (Leiden: E.J. Brill, 1996), pp. 144–153. I have also seen quotations from Genesis relating to Ishmael in several modern Muslim works on the prophets in Indonesia.

8. The Arabic text was first translated by A. Mingana (Manchester, UK: University Press, 1922). One can also consult an edited version of Mingana's translation by N. A. Newman, *The Early Christian-Muslim Dialogue: A Collection of Documents from the First Three Islamic Centuries (632–900 A.D.), Translations with Commentary* (Hatfield, PA: Interdisciplinary Biblical Research Institute, 1995).

9. Newman, pp. 617–618.

10. Harry G. Dorman, *Toward Understanding Islam* (New York: Bureau of Publications Teachers' College, Columbia University, 1948), p. 22.

11. *Janji-janji yang Terlupakan: Ismael Selayang Pandang dari Alkitab* (*The Forgotten Promises: Ishmael from a Biblical Perspective*). Privately published in Bandung, Indonesia, 1998. My purpose in that book was to persuade Indonesian Christians to look at Muslims through the positive and constructive lens of the Ishmael promises in Genesis. By doing so I hoped to reduce prejudice and fear on the part of Christians in the midst of the religious conflicts Indonesia has gone through in the last five years. Interestingly, one hundred students from an Islamic university read my book. They did not agree with all of my conclusions, yet they were surprised that a Christian could write so positively about Hagar and Ishmael.

12. Literally, Hagar "looked with contempt upon her mistress." I have never found a statement in the Islamic tradition which lays any blame on Hagar. Yet, is it not true that two wives in the same household is a recipe for rivalry in which both parties can easily be at fault?

13. From the Hebrew, *yishma'e'l*, which is the imperfect tense of the verb *shema'* ("hear") plus the subject *'el* (God). Essentially it means "God hears" or "God will hear." The name "Samuel" is the perfect tense of the same verbal construction.

14. For centuries Christians have taken this verse to mean that Ishmael and his descendants will be barbarians (cf. Bate, pp. 148–155 for an example from the modern era). But if that is what God means to convey then why does Hagar rejoice after hearing this prophetic oracle in 16:13? For modern readers "wild ass" or "wild donkey" conveys a negative image. But Job 39:5–8 provides God's own description of a wild ass that helps us understand the phrase in question here in Genesis 16:12. In Job, God describes the wild ass as an animal that loves freedom, that avoids cities and noisy settled areas, and that roams about in search of food. This is an apt picture of a Bedouin life-style. When this imagery is applied to Ishmael it means that he will live

like a wild donkey, namely a Bedouin life style marked by independence and no-madism.

15. "Be at odds with" is not the only translation that is possible for the Hebrew, *al-peney*, which literally means, "in the face of." According to the standard Brown, Dri-ver and Briggs, *A Hebrew and English Lexicon of the Old Testament* (Oxford, UK: Clarendon, 1975), p. 818, the term can also mean "in the presence of" or possibly "to the east of." For these last two translations see the King James Version and the New American Standard Bible translations of the original Hebrew text of Genesis. This leaves open the possibility that the Bible does not automatically predestine the de-scendants of Ishmael and the descendants of Abraham's grandson, Israel (Jacob) to live in a state of hostility. For example, note that Jether the Ishmaelite married the sis-ter of David, King of Israel, and that Obil the Ishmaelite took care of King David's camels (cf. 1 Chronicles 2:17, 27:30).

16. The name, *'el roî* means "the God who sees."

17. "He brought him [Abraham] outside and said, 'Look towards heaven and count the stars, if you are able to count them.' Then he said to him, 'So shall your descen-dants be.'"

18. God makes several promises with Abraham and uses the word "covenant" (*berît*) to describe them (Gen. 15:18, 17:2, 4, 7). God promises to bless and protect Abraham, to make his name great, to make him fruitful, to cause nations and kings to descend from him, and most importantly, to make him the channel of spiritual bless-ing for all nations and peoples of the earth (Gen.12:1–3; 17:2–6; 18:18; 22:17–18). Furthermore, God describes this as an "eternal covenant" for Abraham and his off-spring after him (17:7–8). Yet, this covenant with Abraham's "offspring" needs to be qualified within the context of all God's statements, especially, Genesis 17:19, 21, 21:12, 26:4, and 28:13–14. These verses confine to Isaac and Jacob and their descen-dants the essential aspect of covenant–blessing to the nations.

19. (Cairo: al-Halabi 1968) Vol 1, pp. 37–40, quoted in Lewis Scudder, "A Study of the Biblical Foundation for Christian Witness among the Muslims for the RCA To-day." In *Minutes of the General Synod of the Reformed Church of America*. Vol. 70 (Grand Rapids, MI: Reformed Church of America, 1990), p. 408, n.1.

20. Or "make him fruitful and cause him to be multiplied" (cf. with the Abrahamic promise in 17:6). The Hebrew verbal forms here relating to Ishmael are Hiphil causatives and signify that God guarantees that Ishmael and his descendants will achieve this promise. Here it is interesting to compare the United Nations population statistics cited by Samuel Huntington, pp. 116–117, which shows the amazing growth rates of Muslim majority countries.

21. This question was raised in 1829 by an Anglican scholar-priest by the name of Charles Forster as Clinton Bennett recounts in a significant article entitled, "Is Isaac Without Ishmael Complete? A Nineteenth Century Debate Revisited." *Islam and Christian Muslim Relations* 2(1), pp. 42–55, 1991.

22. These are what Hebrew grammarians describe as Hiphil causative verbal forms. It is interesting to note in this regard that according to the statistics compiled by the United Nations, the growth rate of Muslim majority nations is considerably faster than non-Muslim states, including the third world (Huntington, pp. 116–117).

23. God promised Abraham: "I will make you exceedingly fruitful; and I will make nations of you, and kings shall come from you."

24. If we apply the "great nation" promise to Muslims, it would appear to include Arab Muslims but not Indonesians, Pakistanis, and Muslims of other ethnic groups. However, this overlooks the inclusive multi-ethnic nuance in the Hebrew *gôy gedol* (great nation). In Egypt, Israel became a "great nation" (Gen. 46:3; Ex. 1:9) but "a mixed multitude" accompanied them during the exodus (Ex. 12:38). Jeremiah, the "prophet to the nations" (1:5), provides the clearest example of the multi-ethnic possibilities in the term *gôygedol* in his references to Babylon. Interestingly, in 6:22 he refers to Babylon as a "great nation" from the "north land." Elsewhere, Jeremiah describes this "great nation" of Babylon as "all the families (*mishpakhôt*–cf. with Gen.12:3) of the north" (25:9) and "all the kings of the north" (25:26). These references indicate that Babylon is a multi-ethnic entity [cf. R. K. Harrison on the "composite nature" of the Babylonian empire in *Jeremiah & Lamentations: An Introduction and Commentary* (Downer's Grove, IL: Inter Varsity, 1973), p. 125]. Similarly, when the Muslims burst out of the confines of the Arabian peninsula in the seventh century A.D., they began as an ethnic Arab entity. Eventually, they established a multi-ethnic community built on an Arab religious, political, and cultural foundation. In short, they established a "great nation."

25. Abu 'Abdallah Muammad b. Isma'il al-Bukhari, *The Translation of the Meanings of Sahih Al-Bukhari*. Vol. 4. Muhammad Muhsin Khan, trans. (Beirut, Lebanon: Dar Al-Arabia, 1985), pp. 379–382.

26. Literally, "the matter was evil in his eyes."

27. Surely God is not supporting the shrillness and the lack of mercy in Sarah's tone of voice. Here Abraham displays a father's affection for his son and deep concern for Hagar. But on the other hand, Sarah's feeling that Ishmael might grow up to be a competing rival for her son may have some truth in it, and it is at this point that God, in the broader concerns of his providence for both sons of Abraham, permits Sarah to have her way. There will be another time and place for God to work on Sarah's harshness.

28. The word "named" cannot be understood in a strictly literal sense because Ishmael is called "son of Abraham"in many verses in Genesis and elsewhere in the Bible (Gen. 25:9, 12, 1 Chron. 1:28, Gal. 4:22). "Named" can only be connected with God's comments in Genesis 17:19 and 21: "But my covenant I will establish with Isaac."

29. This verse proves that Ishmael is a true "son of Abraham."

30. In the original Hebrew text, the phrase "along with the child" is the last of several phrases in this verse, and is not sequentially connected to the phrase "placed on her shoulder." We would make better sense of this passage if we followed the New International Version translation of the Hebrew text: "Early the next morning Abraham took some food and a skin of water and gave them to Hagar. He set them on her shoulders and then sent her off with the boy. . . ." This translation follows the order of the phrases

31. The translation "cast" (Heb. *salakh*) him under a bush" is inaccurate. The same word for "cast" is used in other biblical verses describing the action of lowering a dead person into a grave (cf., 2 Sam. 18:17; 2 Kg. 13:21; Jer. 41:9). Thus a better way of saying this phrase is Hagar, "placed" or "lay" Ishmael under a bush.

32. The phrase, "And God heard" or *wayishma' elohîm* in Hebrew, contains the long form of Ishmael's name, *yishma'e'l*. This wordplay on Ishmael's name is all the more remarkable because Genesis 21 never mentions Ishmael's name directly. I believe that this play on words underscores Ishmael's importance in the plan of God.

33. We can determine the location of biblical Paran in 1 Kings 11:17–18. These verses state that when Hadad the Edomite fled to Egypt, he departed from the land of Edom and passed through Midian and Paran. This indicates that Paran lay to the west of Edom going towards Egypt.

34. Martin Luther, *Lectures on Genesis, Chapters 21–25*. Vol. 4 of *Luther's Works*, Jaroslav Pelikan, ed. (St. Louis, MO: Concordia, 1964), p. 46.

35. Louis Berkhof, *Systematic Theology* (Edinburgh, UK: Banner of Truth Trust, 1976), p. 168.

Part Two

MUSLIM REFLECTIONS

Chapter Six

CURRENT CONTRIBUTIONS OF RELIGIONS TO WORLD PEACE

Osman Zümrüt
Dean, Professor of the History of Islam
Ondokoz Mayis University, Turkey

"All ye who believe! Enter fully into peace" (al-Baqara [2]:208).

When we talk about peace, we think of tranquility, order, calm, security, and normalcy, and also of development of justice and respect for the basic human rights of others. When we think of lack of peace, we think of disturbance, disorder, insecurity, abnormal conditions, violence and war, underdevelopment, oppression, injustice and violation of human rights. With this definition of peace, we can decide what kind of world we live in today.

Although we are very advanced in science and technology today, we cannot say the same thing in terms of peace, justice and the fulfillment of basic human rights to all on the globe. As stated by scholars who participated in the Parliament of World's Religions, held in Chicago in 1993, our present world is experiencing a fundamental crisis, a crisis in global economy, global ecology, global morality, and global politics. The lack of a grand vision, the tangle of unresolved problems, and too little sense for the commonwealth are seen everywhere. As a result of these enormous problems, hundreds of millions of human beings in underdeveloped, developing and even developed countries increasingly suffer from unemployment, poverty, hunger, and destruction of their families, and violation of basic human rights. There are tensions between the sexes and generations. Children die, kill, and are killed. It is becoming increasingly difficult to live together peacefully in our cities because of social, racial, and ethnic conflicts, the abuse of drugs, organized crime, and even anarchy. Even neighbors often live in fear of one another. In addition to these individual and social crises, the excessive militarization, nuclear weapons, and the probability of nuclear war threaten us.[1]

Do human beings who are created in the image of God (Gen. 1:27) and who were breathed into with God's spirit (Sād [38]:72) deserve to live in such a world? I do not think so. As believers, whatever our beliefs, we need to strongly declare that it need not be. The call for world-wide peace, based on justice, and the preservation of creation has become the watchword for this age, and it applies equally to religious and non-religious people. The present tension in the world must be eliminated by eliminating its causes—injustice, racism, exploitation of developing countries, etc.[2] All responsible people including Muslims, Christians, and Jews should agree on this. And since Muslims, Christians and Jews make up over half of the world's population, the principles they adopt, and how they treat each other will affect the whole world.

Next we should ask the following question of ourselves: Shall we continue to live in the world which is pictured above, or create a new world where everyone will have basic human rights and will be happy? Of course, our religious traditions compel us to live in a peaceful world. So then how can we solve these immense problems? My answer to this question is to turn back to the teachings of religions and put them into our daily lives.

In fact, when we examine the rules of the great world religions, we see that religions consider humankind as one family. They teach us to be kind and generous, not to live for only ourselves, but also to serve others, never forgetting the children, the aged, the poor, the suffering, the disabled and the lonely. The following golden rule from major world religions indicates this fact:

Hinduism: "This is the sum of duty. Do not do to others what would cause you pain if done to you" (Mahabbarata 5.15.17).

Buddhism: "Hurt not others in ways that you would find hurtful" (Udanavarga 5:18).

Confucianism: "It is the maxim of loving kindness (jin): Do not unto others what you would not have them do unto you" (Anaclets Rongo 15:23).

Judaism: "What is hateful to you, do not to your fellow man. That is the entire Law; all the rest is commentary" (Talmud, Shabbat 31 a).

Christianity: "Always treat others as you would like them to treat you; that is the meaning of the Law and the Prophets" (Mt. 7:12).

Islam: "No one of you is a believer until he loves for his brother that which he loves for himself" (The 42 Traditions of An-Nawawi).

African Traditional Religion: "What you give (or do) to others these will give (or do) to you in return" (Rwandan Proverb).[3]

As seen above, religions want their followers to be generous, kind and responsible to others which is the basic requirement of peace in society. Although they differ greatly in faith and prayer systems, they say similar things about the peace of humankind. In fact, almost all religions seek to liberate the individual from sin, from hatred, from preoccupation with material things, and from the oppression of others. Also various religions strive to show faith in God, or the Absolute, or the Transcendent through prayer, spiritual reflection, meditation and sacred readings. All these things lead us to appreciate deeper truths and to see our relationship to our Creator and to fellow humankind.

Thirty years ago, the leaders of all the major world religions (221 delegates at Kyoto, Japan in October 1970 A.D.) stated as follows:

As we gathered together in concern for the overriding subject of peace, we discovered that the things which unite us are more important that the things which divide us. We found that in common we possessed:

1. a conviction of the fundamental unity of the human family, of the equality and dignity of all human beings;
2. a feeling for the inviolability of the individual and his conscience;
3. a feeling for the value of the human community;
4. a recognition that might does not make right, that human power is not sufficient unto itself and is not absolute;
5. the belief that love, compassion, selflessness and the power of the spirit and of inner sincerity ultimately have greater strength than hate, enmity and self-interest;
6. a feeling of obligation to stand on the side of the poor and oppressed against the rich and the oppressor;
7. deep hope that ultimately good will be victorious.[4]

Although religions seek to promote peace in the heart of the individual and societies at large, Islam among these has a special place in promoting peace in the world. Islam presents itself as a universalistic religion,[5] and sees all humankind as a family irrespective of their color, origin, nationality, sex, and socio-economic status.[6] Islam does not see any problem with establishing good relationships with the followers of other faiths. Contrary, it compels Muslims to work together in good deeds. The Qur'an reads, "Help ye one another in righteousness and piety, but help ye not one another in sin and rancor: Fear Allah, for Allah is strict in punishment" (al-Mā'ida [5]:2).

If the principles of Islam were practiced in our modern world, I strongly believe that most of the world's problem would be solved. The principles concerning world peace can be summarized as follows:

The dignity of human beings: Islam, first of all, commands Muslims to respect and believe in the dignity of human beings. Allah himself honored human beings in many ways. The Qur'an says: "When I fashioned him and breathed into him of My spirit, fall ye down in prostration unto him" (Sād [38]:72). "And behold, We said to the angels: 'Bow down to Adam:' and they bowed down" (al-Baqara [2]:34). "We have indeed created man in the best of molds" (al-Tīn [95]:4). Again the Qur'an gives a great importance to the life of a human being irrespective of his/her belief. We read in the Qur'an: "Whoever kills a human being, except as a punishment for murder or other villainy in the land, shall be looked upon as though he had killed all mankind; and whoever saves a human life shall be regarded as though he had saved all mankind" (al-Mā'ida [5]:32). How can a believer kill a person in light of this verse, if he really believes in God?

Relationship with unbelievers: There are certain passages from the Qur'an that seem to be biased against Jews, Christians, and other non-Muslims. For instance, "Let not the Believers take for friends or helpers unbelievers rather than believers: if any do that, in nothing will there be help from Allah except by way of precaution, that ye may guard yourselves from them" (Al 'Imrān [3]:28). "0 ye who believe! take not My enemies and yours as friends."[7] However, when we explain those verses in light of historical developments, we see that the Qur'an does not forbid Muslims to establish good relationship with unbelievers. A well-known scholar of Islam Yusuf al-Qaradavi, evaluating these verses, first argues that, contrary to common belief, "not to take opponents as friends" refers specially to non-Muslims who actively work against Islam and Muslims—not to those who live peacefully with Muslims. Second, the enmity which is prohibited is not the relationship of cordiality, but rather enmity shown to those who harm Muslims and oppose the call and spread of Islam. The reason for forbidding friendship with polytheists was twofold: These people denied Islam, and they unjustly expelled the Prophet and the Muslims from their homes. Thus Muslims may take as friends those unbelievers who do not oppress Muslims and destroy their faith. The Qur'an says, "Allah forbids you not, with regard to those who fight you not for [your] faith nor drive you out of your homes, from dealing kindly and justly with them" (al-Mumtahana [60]:8). Furthermore, Islam allows Muslims to marry the women of the People of the Book. This also proves that friendship between Muslims and non-Muslims is allowed, for married life requires peaceful and affectionate relationships.[8]

Regard for the differences of faith: Since differences of religion among human beings are a matter of divine decision, it is not the duty of Muslims to call non-believers to account for their disbelief, nor to punish those who go astray for their errors. This world is not a place of judgment, for on the Last Day Allah will call them to account; on that day He will requite them. Allah says: "If they do wrangle with thee, say, Allah knows best what it is ye are doing: Allah will judge between you on the Day of Judgment concerning the matters in which ye differ."[9] Even some Muslim scholars, for example Muhamed Talbi, argue that "the cornerstone of all human rights is religious liberty, for religion, which is the "explanation of the meaning of life and how to live accordingly," is the most fundamental and comprehensive of human institutions."[10] The Qur'an states clearly that compulsion is incompatible with religion: "There should be no compulsion in religion" (al-Baqara [2]:256). Again Talbi writes "To the best of my knowledge, among all the revealed texts, only the Qur'an stresses religious liberty in such a precise and unambiguous way: faith, to be true and reliable faith, absolutely needs to be a free and voluntary act."[11]

Giving value to good people in different religions: Rejecting exclusivism and election, the Qur'an repeatedly recognizes the existence of good people in other communities—Jews, Christians and Sabians—just as it recognizes the people of faith in Islam. The Qur'an says: "Those who believe [in the Qur'an]. And those who follow the Jewish [scriptures], and the Christians and the Sabians, any who believe in Allah and the Last Day, and work righteousness, shall have their reward with their Lord, on them shall be no fear, nor shall they grieve"(al-Baqara [2]:62; al-Mā'ida [5]:69). Thus, the Qur'an accepts the positive values of different religions and communities. It urges Muslims to help each other in good deeds. It says: "Help ye one another in righteousness and piety. But help ye not one another in sin and rancor" (al-Mā'ida [5]:2). In another verse, "To each is a goal to which Allah turns him; then strive together [as in a race] towards all that is good" (al-Baqara [2]:148,177).[12]

From all of these principles brought by Islam we can say that Islam is a religion of peace. In fact, one of the literal meanings of the word Islam is "peace." This signifies that one can achieve the real peace of body and mind only through submission and obedience to Allah. Such a life of obedience brings peace of heart and establishes real peace in society at large.

NOTES

1. See "The Principles of a Global Ethic" and "The Parliament of the World's Religions: Declaration toward Global Ethic," in *Yes to a Global Ethic*, ed. Hans Küng (New York: The Continuum Publishing, 1996), pp. 9–11.

2. Karl Wolfgang Tröger, "Peace and Islam: In Theory and Practice," *Islam and Christian-Muslim Relations*, vol. 1, no. 1 (1990), p. 12.

3. Francis Arinze, "Interreligious Dialogue at the Service of Peace," *Islamo-cihristiana*, 13 (1987), p. 4.

4. Leoanard Swidler, "Interreligious and Interideological Dialogue: The Matrix for All Systematic Reflection Today," *Toward a Universal Theology of Religion*, ed. Leoanard Swidler (Maryknoll, New York: Orbis Books, 1988), pp. 29–30.

5. See al-A'rāf [7]:158, al-Furqān [25]:1; al-Anbiyā [21]:107.

6. The Qur'an says: "0 mankind, We have created you from a male and female, and set you up as nations and tribes so you may recognize one another. The noblest among you with God is that one of you who best performs his duty; God is Aware, Informed" (al-Hurjurāt [49]:13).

7. Al-Mumtahana [60]:1; see for others al-Nisā' [4]:139,144; al-Mā'ida [5]:51; al-Tawba [9]:23.

8. Yusuf al-Qaradavi, *Non-Muslims in the Islamic Society*, translated by Khalil Muhammad Hamad and Sayed M. Ali Shah (Indianapolis: American Trust, 1985), pp. 44–45.

9. Al-Hajj (22):68–69; Al-Qaradawi, *Non-Muslims*, pp. 31–32.

10. Mohamed Talbi, "Religious Liberty: A Muslim Perspective," in *Muslims in Dialogue: The Evolution of A Dialogue*, ed. Leonard Swidler (Lewiston, The Edven: Mellen Press, 1992), p. 469.

11. Ibid., p. 470.

12. Fazlur Rahman, *Major Themes of the Qur'an* (Chicago: Bibliotheca Islamica, 1980), pp. 162–70.

Chapter 7

RELIGIOUS PLURALISM AS AN OPPORTUNITY FOR LIVING TOGETHER IN DIVERSITY

Mahmut Aydin
Assistant Professor, History of Religions and
Inter-religious Dialogue
Ondokoz Mayis University, Turkey

As is well known, since the 1960's we have been witnessing the beginning of a "new age" in our relationship with people of other faiths. This period is called a "paradigm-shift" by Hans Küng,[1] "the second axial period" by E. Cousins[2] and "the age of global dialogue" by L. Swidler.[3] In this age, as Swidler underlines, we have passed from the age of monologue to the age of dialogue. In our contemporary world, in which religious and cultural pluralism is an unavoidable reality, we are entering into a relationship with people of other faiths in every moment and in every place. It is even argued that in this age entering into dialogue with the "other" is not only becoming widespread but also becoming a necessity for a peaceful world in which all people can live together while keeping their differences. For, as Macquarrie rightly states, dialogue between the followers of different religious traditions is a civilized way of resolving conflicts and problems that they have among them, as opposed to the methods of violence and coercion.[4]

Within this context, this paper will discuss whether the religious pluralism that has begun to come out both as an intellectual and practical response to the current religious diversity and as a contribution to the coming together of members of various religious traditions under "inter-religious dialogue" may provide an opportunity for our living together within the diversity of our faiths. We will do this by first of all highlighting how religions have been used to justify some human evils in the course of history in terms of their absolute truth claims. Secondly, we will elaborate the main arguments of religious pluralism. And finally, we will try to show how the main arguments of religious pluralism can save religious traditions from the hands of those who use them to justify or bless human evils and can thus lead us to live with people of other faiths in harmony.

THE ROLE OF ABSOLUTE TRUTH CLAIMS OF RELIGIONS IN SUPPORT OF HUMAN EVILS

As is well known, in the course of history the absolute truth claims of the world religions have sometimes been used to validate and intensify many human conflicts and many violent episodes of persecution and repression. This occurs because these truth claims take precedence over everything else, and they justify anything in order to defend their existence. When we look at the history of the world, the absolute truth claims of world religions have been used to rationalize a number of great evils. These evils have even been blessed by those who have done them. They do these human evils in the name of God or for the sake of their religious traditions. Of course, there were also a number of other factors—namely, political, economic and cultural—that led to these human evils. Some of these great human evils have threatened the entire world's peace by causing conflict and enmity among the followers of different world religions and sometimes even among adherents of the same religion. Here, we would like to highlight some of these great human evils in order to show how the claim of unique superiority of one particular religious tradition as the one and only true faith was used to bless them in the course of history.

THE CHURCH'S PERSECUTION OF NON-CHRISTIANS

During the early Christianization of the Roman Empire and Europe in the fourth to eighth centuries, the Church persecuted and oppressed those who were not Christian. As is well known, after the crucifixion of Jesus, Christianity began to spread to the Roman Empire through the mission work of Paul and the early Christian communities. In the first years, the authorities of the Roman Empire did not interfere with Paul or the other Christian preachers. But after Christians increased day by day and the Christian population of the Roman Empire became a political threat to the state, the Roman authorities began to persecute Christians.

However, Christianity became the official religion of the Roman Empire in the fourth century, and the situation reversed. This time the Christian authorities, thanks to the power of the Roman Empire, began to persecute and oppress those who had persecuted and oppressed them. According to some modern researchers, after Christianity gained the status of the official religion of the Roman Empire, the spread of Christianity in the Roman Empire and Europe was no longer a peaceful spread of the faith among willing converts, but a violent suppression of the existing local Roman cults and natural religions. In this period, as Ramsay MacMullen underlines, those who had begged for mercy from the Roman authorities became the persecutors who were asked for mercy. It became increasingly necessary to be a member of the church if one was to prosper in a profession and increasingly dangerous to remain outside the church, because laws were passed in this period restricting the imperial civil service to Christians. Militant monks and Church authorities led mobs to destroy pagan shrines and temples. Also in this period many non-Christian books were publicly burned. Again according to MacMullen a number of prominent non-Christians were beheaded or crucified by the Church authorities. Because of the great human evils of the Christian authorities in this period, MacMullen argues that the pagan religions were much more tolerant than Christianity.[5]

The Church continued to persecute through the second half of the twentieth century. After Christianity became the official religion of the Roman Empire, the Church Fathers widened the scope of the axiom of the *Extra Ecclesiam Nulla Salus* by applying it not only to the Christian heretics but also to those who belonged to other religions. Thus, it was stressed that those who had heard the message of the Gospel but had not become Christians were guilty because of their rejection of the Gospel message.[6] This traditional dogma has been understood literally by some Christian authorities up through the 1960's. During this period, they have sometimes persecuted and oppressed non-Christians and then justified and blessed these kind of human evils by arguing that they did them in the name of God and Jesus Christ in order to proclaim the Gospel to the whole world and to baptize all nations.

ANTI-SEMITISM

As is well known, for a very long time some Christian authorities held the Jews responsible for the death of Jesus Christ. This charge of the Church led Christians to regard Jews as the enemies of God. Since, according to the traditional Christian belief, Jesus Christ was the incarnate son of God on the earth, killing Jesus was considered equal to killing God. Because of this supposition, Christians treated Jews very badly. Let me give you a number of examples that show the ill treatment of Jews by Christians. According to one story, "the Jews of Norwich, England used the blood of murdered Christian children in their Passover bread and this blood libel spread throughout Europe, unleashing a fresh wave of violent persecution."[7] According to another story, in 1182 A.D the French king cancelled all Christian debts to Jewish creditors. Apart from these stories, in the fourth Lateran Council (1215 A.D.) the Church authorities dictated that Jews must wear special clothes in order to be distinguished from the Christians.[8]

This mentality continued in the course of history in many places where Christians and Jews came into contact with each other. For example, during the Christian Reconquista of Spain especially in Cordoba Christian authorities killed not only Muslims but also Jews. Since, as we have said above they held them as responsible for the death of Christ.[9] This sort of anti-Semitism reached its climax in the 20th century when a few million Jews were massacred by the Nazis during the Second World War.[10] However, after the 1960's especially during the Second Vatican Council the magisterium officially decreed that not all the Jews but only those Jews who caused the death of Christ were responsible for his death, and they urged Christians to strive to overcome prejudice and search for justice and peace in their homes, communities, and work places.[11]

THE CRUSADES

The wars which were inaugurated by the Church against the Muslim East are known as the Crusades because of their religious character. As is well known, in 1095 A.D. Pope Urban II urged all Christians to come together around the cross in order to take back Jerusalem from the hands of Muslims. Because, according to this Pope, it would not be possible for Christians to observe their pilgrimage as long as Jerusalem was in the hands of Muslims. The Pope also declared that Christians had to recapture Jerusalem in order to facilitate or expedite the return of Christ.[12] So, as is argued by some historians, although there were various reasons for the Crusades, the primary reason was religious. For this reason, the Christian soldiers who participated in these wars believed that they observed a religious duty by killing the Muslims. Because of this belief, when the Crusaders captured Jerusalem they massacred the Muslims who lived in there. They believed that the more Muslims they killed the more pious their reward would be. According to some historians, because of the religious character of the Crusades, the response to Pope Urban II's call was greater than he had expected. One itinerant preacher who lived in that time stated:

> It was an age of visions: and Peter was thought to be a visionary. Medieval man was convinced that the Second Coming was at hand. He must repent while yet

there was time and must go out and do good. The Church taught that sin could be expiated by pilgrimage and prophecies declared that the Holy Land must be recovered for the faith before Christ could come again. Further, to ignorant minds the distinction between Jerusalem and the New Jerusalem was not very clearly defined. Many of Peter's hearers believed that he was promising to lead them out of their present miseries to the land flowing with milk and honey of which the scripture spoke. The journey would be hard; there were the legions of Antichrist to be overcome. . . .[13]

THE JEWISH NOTION OF A CHOSEN PEOPLE

A central feature of Judaism is the belief that Israel is God's chosen people. Because of this chosenness, the Jewish people have believed that God has given them a historic mission to bear divine truth to humanity. According to this central doctrine of Judaism the Jewish people have these responsibilities: "Israel is obligated to keep God's statutes and observe his laws, and in doing so, the nation will be able to persuade others that there is only one universal God. By carrying out this task, Israel is to be a light to the nations."[14] Because of this belief concerning the course of history, the Jewish people contend that they are God's chosen people and partners in a special covenant. Their mission is to be a light to the nations. In this sense they stand in a unique relationship with God. However, this does not lead to the quest to convert others to Judaism, since Judaism is not a missionary religion but a national faith. However, being the chosen people of God gives rise to a sense of pride in having been born into the Jewish fold.

JIHÂD [HOLY WAR]

As is well known, Muslims have in the course of history sometimes fought the "others" in the name of God in order to spread their own beliefs to them. Muslims have stated that there are three options for those who belong to other faiths. Either they convert to Islam or pay the tax called "*jizya*" or are killed. This Muslim attitude has depended on the verse that is called "the verse of the sword." In this verse, Muslims are called to "kill the idolaters whererever they find them, take them [as captives], besiege them, and lie in wait for them at every point of observation. If they repent afterwards, perform the prayer and pay the alms, then release them. . . ."[15] When we look at Islamic History, Muslim armies invaded the lands of non-Muslims, arguing that they were doing this in the name of God in order to keep the order of this verse. However, by doing this they have forgotten those verses which call Muslims to be tolerant and just towards the other. For example, another place the Qur'an urges Muslims to do justice to those who do fight with them and not to expel them from their land.[16]

Within this context, when we look at the process of the institutionalization of the teaching of the Prophet Muhammad in Islamic history, Muslim scholars and especially commentators and jurists have attempted to end any toleration and positive attitude of Muslims towards others by abrogating those verses which encourage Muslims to behave in a good manner to the others. For example, some commentators argued that the verses "Do not dispute with the people of the Book save in the fairer way; except for those of them who are evildoers" and "We believe in what has been sent down to us and what has been sent down to you; Our God and your God are one"[17] were abrogated by the sword verse.[18] Thus, Muslim scholars narrowed the meaning by understanding it as an armed struggle with those who are non-Muslims in order to try to convert them to Islam. As a consequence of this narrower understanding of Jihad, the world in classical Islamic thought was divided into two categories—namely, the house of war (dâr al-harb) and the house of Islam (dâr al-Islam). In doing so, the co-operation and collaboration of Muslims with others has been hindered. Islam began to be understood as a religion of war or the sword instead of a religion of peace, and before the 1960's the relationship of Muslims towards others was shaped by an understanding in which the non-Muslims "either convert to Islam or are to be killed." Concerning this point, M. Khadduri underlines that when this narrowed understanding of jihad is abandoned, then peace will be possible in Islam.[19]

As we have seen up to this point, the absolute truth claims of religions have played very significant roles in some human evils that have occurred throughout history. Even today in the first years of the 21st century when we look at the world we can see that there are still a number of conflicts in which religions have played a great role. This can be noted in all of the following examples: between Jewish Israelis and Muslim Palestinians, between Christians Serbs and Muslim Kosovans, between Muslim Indonesians and Christian East Timorese, between the Muslim north and the Christian south in Sudan, between Christian Protestant and Catholic parties in Northern Ireland. We can increase the number of events mentioned, but these are sufficient to show how religions have been used to justify and bless the human evils that have been caused primarily for political reasons.

Concerning this point, I would like to indicate that my objective is not to show that religions themselves have a high potential to cause conflict in order to threaten world peace, because when we look at the main teachings of the world religions, especially the five major religions, we can see that all of them urge their followers to do to others what they would like done to themselves. Sometimes this ethical principle is articulated positively—that is in instructing people to act in a certain way. Other times, however, it is articulated negatively—that is, warning against selfish behavior.[20] Furthermore, the major world religions invite their adherents to love their neighbors as they love themselves. Concerning this principle, we cannot love our neighbors unless we are ready to dialogue with them. As Knitter points out, if we do not extend to the others the same care and respect that we would wish for ourselves, we do not really love them. If we enter a relationship with the others presupposing that we have the fullness of God's truth and they have only partial rays of that truth, we will easily view them as less able than we to know the truth or to live moral lives or to know God. With such an attitude we do not really love them.[21]

Concerning the high potential for adherents of different religions to live together peacefully, Hans Küng states that the thesis of Samuel Huntington called the "clash of civilizations" is only a half truth. "For the civilizations and religions have not only high potential for conflict but also a high potential for peace, which they have shown not only in the revolution in Eastern Europe but also in the removal of the dictatorship in the Philippines and the abolition of Apartheid in South Africa."[22] At this point, these questions come to our mind: How have religions that have this very significant ethical teaching been used to justify and bless human evils? Or if the different world religions have a high potential for living together in harmony and peace, how have they been used and still are used to cause conflicts or to justify and bless the conflicts and enmity among their followers?

It seems to me that the answer to these kinds of questions is not easy, since everyone can answer them differently with regard to his/her perspective. According to my view point, the main teachings of the religions do not have any implications that cause human evils or justify and bless them. However, the historical structures and dogmas, which imply that every religion has a unique superiority over the others, have been used to justify and bless human evils, since religions have played "a significant role by blessing both sides in each conflict, and by intensifying the rival loyalties and motivating young men to be willing to kill and to be killed for a sacred cause."[23] Because of this implication of the classical dogmas or conflicting truth claims of religions, it seems to me that we need to reconsider those dogmas, so that they are not used to justify and bless human evils, but that they might instead establish a world in which we may live in a peaceful way within the context of our own particular beliefs. I believe the main arguments of religious pluralism can help us accomplish this goal. I would now like to summarize the main arguments of religious pluralism and then explain how they can be used for a better and more fruitful inter-religious dialogue.

RELIGIOUS PLURALISM AS AN
OPPORTUNITY FOR LIVING TOGETHER

As we have said above, after the second half of the twentieth century religious pluralism, as we have observed today, has emerged both as an intellectual and practical response to the current religious diversity and as a contribution to the facilitation of the coming together of the members of various religious traditions under "inter-religious dialogue." As is well known, instead of arguing that there is only one true and absolute religion, or widening the boundaries of an absolute religion in order to include the followers of other religions, religious pluralism emphasizes the equal validity of every religious traditions to bring their adherents to salvation. In other words, according to the defenders of religious pluralism, there are many true or valid religious paths through which people can be acceptable to God. These defenders of religious pluralism argue that the major world religions are human responses to the Ultimate Reality or God. According to this argument the various religious traditions of our world "each with its own sacred scripture, spiritual practices, forms of religious experience, belief systems, founder or great exemplars, communal memories, cultural expression in ways of life, laws and customs, art forms and so on, taken together as complex historical totalities, constitute different human response to the ultimate transcendent reality to which they all, in their different ways, bear witness."[24]

According to this understanding, all religions try to transform their adherents from ego-centrism to God or Reality-centrism. This is a pluralism which says that all religions point to the same truth, the Ultimate Divine Reality beyond the various images and doctrinal formulations of the diverse faiths. In this argument, Reality is like the Sun, around which revolve the planetary religions.[25] In short, according to this understanding neither this religion nor that religion, or this religious figure nor that religious figure is the only means to salvation, since salvation or being acceptable to God only comes from God, and can be experienced in every religious tradition through various ways or mediators. According to this feature, religious pluralism, for those who adopt it, represents a new attitude in terms of understanding one's own religion and the religions of others.

As we can see, pluralism affirms the plurality of ways through which people can reach God and thus salvation. It does this, as Knitter says, "not because plurality is good in itself but because it is a fact of life and the stuff of relationship."[26] Just as we seek to develop and nurture a relationship among our close friends and colleagues, this pluralistic view also seeks to promote authentic, truly mutual and fruitful relationships between the adherents of different world religions without underestimating or despising their differences.

In the dialogical understanding which pluralism seeks to establish, the followers of different world religions speak honestly with each other and listen to each other authentically. Far from requiring that all people must have the same view, pluralism presumes that the religions are truly diverse, since without genuine diversity dialogue becomes something that we talk to ourselves about in the mirror. In a dialogue process, in which the pluralistic worldview is dominant, the followers of different world religions witness what makes them distinct by trying to show and convince others of the values they have found in their religious traditions. By dong this they are also open to the witness of truth that their dialogue partners make to them. As Knitter states, "this is a mutual, back and forth, co-relationship of speaking and listening, teaching and learning, witnessing and being witnessed to."[27]

According to the pluralistic dialogical worldview, those who participate in the dialogue process will speak their mind and make truth claims to each other without doing so from a theological position that claims that their faith is meant to dominate or absorb or stand in judgment over all other faiths. Religious pluralism's main argument as highlighted above stresses that when we enter into dialogue with the religious others we cannot begin with the idea that our religion holds all the cards or is superior in all respects over the others or has the final norm that will exclude or absorb all other norms. For, as Knitter points out, "just as a relationship between two human beings cannot thrive if one of them claims, before the relationship even begins, to be superior or always to have the final word, so too the relationship constitutive of interfaith dialogue is doomed to failure if one religion claims, *a priori*, general superiority over all others to the extent that it is not willing or able to learn from them."[28]

In the light of all these views, we may conclude that the pluralistic worldview tries to establish an environment of dialogue in which, not the Church, nor Jesus Christ nor Christianity, nor the institutionalized religion of the Prophet Muhammad, but God alone is the center. Also, Christians and Muslims would no longer insist that, in Jesus or in the institutionalized religion of the Prophet Muhammad, they have the only or the final norm for all religious truth. By doing this all believers will come together on the basis of their different experiences of the one Ultimate Reality or God or al-Haqq.

As we have seen up to now, the absolute truth claims of religions have sometimes caused many problems among the followers of different world religions because according to those claims only one religion is the true religion or only one religious figure is the mediator by whom we can reach God. The absolute truth claims of religions limit God to a certain geographic area, a certain history and a certain cultural environment, confining the accessibility of salvation to only a small minority. In this case, the adherents of different world religions begin to argue that only their religion is the true religion and all others are false. So, by doing this, they indicate that all those who belong to false religions must be converted to this one faith—one way or another. This sort of understanding, too, would bring them to clash in order to overcome each other.

It seems to me that the main arguments of religious pluralism, which we have observed above, can help prevent the use of religions in order to justify and bless human evils such as religious wars, persecution of the other and enmity among the followers of different world religions. We can elaborate the benefits of the above arguments of religious pluralism on living together by keeping our differences as follows:

1. The arguments of religious pluralism urge us to view and approach other religious traditions and their followers in such a way that an authentic co-relation can exist among ourselves.
2. The main objective of different world religions should be to maintain a real relationship with each other, to do all one can to keep from cutting off the relationship or harming it by subordinating the adherents of one religious tradition to another.
3. In the process of dialogue, which is shaped by the above arguments of religious pluralism, while we will speak our convictions and our mind clearly and strongly, we will do so in such a way that allows the others to do the same. This principle does not underestimate our faiths, but relativizes them by indicating that just as our faiths are true for us, the faiths of others, too, can be true for them.
4. If religious persons enter into dialogue with the understanding that their particularities are relative and corrigible, they will be more open to the particularities of other religions, understanding them also to be relative and corrigible. Thus, each particularity "may contribute to the process of all understanding each other and the attempt to formulate a mutually agreeable description of the transcendent order or being."[29]
5. So, in the light of these last two points all religions are viewed, from the beginning of the conversation, as not necessarily being equal or the same in their truth claims, but as having equal rights. This means that pluralism does not suppose that all the world religions are the same, but it does argue that all religions are equally valuable in the eyes of their followers in order to bring them to salvation.
6. According to the above main arguments of religious pluralism, if we need to make normative or absolute truth claims in our dialogue with people of other faiths, we will do so in a way that still recognizes and allows our

partners to do likewise. Otherwise that dialogue will look like a dialogue that occurs between a cat and a mouse.

7. This point indicates that in the dialogue process, which we shape in the light of the main arguments of religious pluralism, we are open to the possibility that our normative claims may be corrected or "formed" by what our dialogue partners have to say.

8. Since religious pluralism does not presuppose that one particular religion has absolute truth, we open ourselves to share the truths of others and at the same time we will give an opportunity to others to know our truth in order to reap benefit from it. For, thanks to religious pluralism, we feel that we do not need to limit ourselves to the sources of our faith alone.

9. Lastly, according to the arguments of religious pluralism, in our dialogical age, as the followers of different world religions, we have the following two tasks. (1) Entering into dialogue with people of other faiths without making absolute claims concerning the superiority of our faiths to others. For, only by doing this can we save our faiths from the misuse of those who create the human evils, which we observed at the beginning. (2) In our day, as adherents of various religious traditions, we need to channel our energies into solving the common human problems that threaten our future on the earth. In order to observe these two points, first of all, we must avoid negative and limiting attitudes towards other religions and their followers. Secondly, we must evade both a narrow fundamentalism and a bland universalism. Thirdly, we must be true to our spiritual heritage, for this is the source of our power and our gift to the world. Fourthly, we need to take every effort to ground ourselves in our own traditions and at the same time open ourselves to other religious traditions.

In short, when we take into account what we have said here, we can argue that the reconsideration or modification of the absolute truth claims of world religions, in the light of the main arguments of religious pluralism, may prevent religions from being used by us in order to justify and bless our ill-treatment or our negative attitude towards the other. Otherwise, it seems to me that we cannot protect ourselves from barbarous and self-indulgent abuses of our own absolute truth claims. Just as we need someone else to tell us when our breath is bad, so we need others to tell us when absolute truth claims have become ideological abuse. So, through entering into dialogue with others we need to open ourselves to the views of others who see the world differently than we do, who can therefore look at our truth differently and tell us not only what it looks like, but how it affects them.

NOTES

1. See Hans Küng, "Paradigm Change in Theology: A Proposal for Discussion," in Küng & Tracy, eds., *Theology and Paradigm Change* (New York: Crossroads, 1989), pp. 3–33.

2. See, Ewert Cousins, "Judaism-Christianity-Islam: Facing Modernity Together," *Journal of Ecumenical Studies*, 30/3–4 (1993), pp. 417–425.

3. Leonard Swidler, "The Age of Global Dialogue," in Jacques Waardenburg, ed., *Islam and Christianity: Mutual Perceptions Since the Mid-20th Century* (Louvain: Peeters, 1998), pp. 269–292.

4. John Macquarrie, "Dialogue among the World Religions," *The Expository Times*, 108/6 (1997), p. 167.

5. Ramsay MacMullen, *Christianity and Paganism in the Fourth to Eighth Centuries* (New Haven: Yale University Press, 1997), p. 25.

6. Francis A. Sullivan, *Salvation Outside the Church: Tracing the History of the Catholic Church Response* (New York: Paulist Press, 1992), p. 20; Mahmut Aydin, *Modern Western Christian Theological Understandings of Muslims Since the Second Vatican Council* (Unpublished Ph.D. thesis, Birmingham: The University of Birmingham, 1998), p. 12.

7. John Hick, "Religion, Violence and Global Conflict: A Christian Proposal," *Global Dialogue*, 2/1(2000), p. 2.

8. J. Neuner and J. Dupuis, *The Christian Faith: In the Doctrinal Documents of the Catholic Church* (Bangalore: Theological Publication in India, 1996), p. 426.

9. As is well known, the Ottoman Empire welcomed the migrating Jews, protected them against oppression of Christians, granted them communal autonomy, and tolerated their religious practices. Joseph R. Hacker, "Ottoman Policy toward the Jews and Jewish Attitudes toward the Ottomans during the Fifteenth Century," in Benjamin Braude and Bernard Lewis, eds., *Christians and Jews In the Ottoman Empire* (New York: Holmes & Meier Pub., 1982), pp. 117–126.

10. Hick, p. 2.

11. See, "Declaration On the Relation of the Church To Non-Christian Religions," in Austin Flannery, ed., *Vatican Council II: The Conciliar and Post Conciliar Documents* (Dublin: Dominican Pub., 1975), pp. 740–742; Lawrence E. Frizzell, "The Catholic Church and the Jewish People: Evaluating the Results of the Second Vatican Council," in Val Ambrose McInnes, ed., *New Visions: Historical and Theological Perspectives on the Jewsih-Christian Dialogue* (New York: Crossroad, 1993), pp. 115–136.

12. See, S. Runciman, *A History of the Crusade* (Cambridge: Cambridge Univ. Press, 1951), I, pp. 5ff.

13. Ibid., p. 12.

14. Dan Cohn-Sherbok, "Judaism and the Copernican Shift in the Universe of Faiths," *Global Dialogue*, 2/1(2000), 35.

15. Al-Tawba [9]:5.

16. Al-Mumtahana [60]:8.

17. Al-'Ankabut [29]:46.

18. Concerning the abrogation of this verse see Ebu'l Fidâ İsmâil Ibn Kesîr, *Tefsir'ul Kur'an'l Azîm* (Beyrut: 1983), III, p. 415; M.Okuyan & M. Öztürk, "Kur'an Verilerine Göre 'Öteki'nin Konumu," Cafer S. Yaran, ed., *Islam ve Öteki* (Istanbul, 2001), pp. 186–188.

19. Majid Khadduri, *War and Peace in the Law of Islam* (Baltimore: Johns Hopkins University Press, 1955), p. 145.

21. For a different version of this ethical principle see, Levililer 19:18; Talmud, *Shabbath*, 31a; Matt 7:12; Luk 6:31; Bukhari *Iman/Faith*, 71.72.

20. Paul F. Knitter, "Five Theses on the Uniqueness of Jesus," in L. Swidler & P. Mojzes, eds., *The Uniqueness of Jesus: A Dialogue with Paul F. Knitter* (Maryknoll: Orbis Books, 1997), p. 6.

22. Hans Küng, "Editorial: Islam-A Challenge to Christianity," Hans Küng and Jürgen Moltmann, eds., *Islam: A Challenge for Christianity* (London: SCM Press, 1994), p.vii.

23. Hick, p. 1.

24. Hick, *The Fifth Dimension: An Exploration of the Spiritual Realm* (Oxford: Oneworld, 1999), p. 77. W. Cantwell Smith terms the historical structures of religions which developed in the course of history as "cumulative tradition" in his *The Meaning and the End of Religion* (Minneapolis: Fortress Press, 1991, first published in 1962), pp. 156–157.

25. Ninnian Smart, *Choosing A Faith* (London: Boyars, 1995), p. 101.

26. Paul Knitter, *Jesus and the Other Names: Christian Mission and Global Responsibility* (Maryknoll: Orbis Books, 1996), p. 17.

27. Ibid., p. 17.

28. Ibid., pp. 17–18.

29. Chester Gillis, *Pluralism: A New Paradigm for Theology* (Louvain: Peeters Press, 1993), p. 60.

Chapter Eight

A COMMON HUMAN AGENDA FOR CHRISTIANS AND MUSLIMS

Mustafa Köylü
Assistant Professor of Religious Education
Ondokoz Mayis University, Turkey

INTRODUCTION

Throughout history, religion has played an important role in the lives of people. In spite of the predictions of some that the time of religion is passing, today we see its importance increasing, rather than lessening. Perhaps the greatest importance for today is whether adherents of differing faiths will continue the threatening postures of the past, or seek to live in peace. Hans Küng writes, "One of the greatest achievements of this century . . . was to bring together nations that had considered themselves hereditary enemies."[1]

This is a positive step in human history, and I believe that this process is nowhere more important than in the relationship between Christians and Muslims. There are at least three reasons for this: (1) In spite of their similarities, Muslims and Christians have been hostile towards and suspicious of each other. The process of mutual understanding has had a good beginning, but it is only a beginning; (2) the two groups together compose nearly half of the world's total population; and (3) together they hold much of the world's resources, and control the lion's share of the world's territory. For example, the Muslim world holds abundant natural resources, while the West has maintained leadership in science and technology. If they could be brought to use these resources jointly, for the benefit of humankind, they could create a world of peace rather than the strife we see today. It can be argued that the future of the world depends mostly on the actions of Muslims and Christians.

Since the 1960s, there have been good developments in inter-religious dialogue between Christians and Muslims. Both sides have worked for mutual understanding, and much has been written on the possibilities of and conditions for continuing dialogue. However, if we want this process to proceed farther, we should be honest and sincere about our limits and motives. Although we try to give credit to each other's faith, every one remains certain that his/her own is best. Instead of trying to find similarities between religions in terms of theology, or trying to accommodate what cannot be accommodated, we should make every effort to work out a common agenda for solving the world's problems.

This paper deals with what can be done together by Christians and Muslims about our common human situation. It consists of three sections: (1) A review of the current state of human affairs, (2) Muslim views regarding addressing the human condition, and (3) Christian views regarding addressing the human condition.

REASONS FOR A COMMON HUMAN AGENDA

While progress in science and technology has brought many blessings to human beings, they have, at the same time, brought certain curses. Perhaps the most pervasive of these curses are a global military industrial complex that demands disproportionate resources and the lack of economic justice in the world.

Wars and conflicts have been inseparable from the history of humankind, and, as Betty A. Reardon points out, "physical or direct violence, particularly military violence, in the twentieth century, appears to be more varied and certainly more destructive than it has ever been."[2] Scholars estimate that from 1480 A.D. to 1940 A.D. there were 244 important wars,[3] but since World War II there have been 149 similar wars.[4] Because of war, some 142 million people have died since the sixteenth century. Of that number, 108 million, or 75 percent, have died during the twentieth century.[5] Overall, according to William Eckhardt's estimation, 73 percent of all war-related deaths since 3000 B.C. have occurred in the twentieth century.[6] Another important feature of twentieth century wars is that most conflicts and deaths have occurred in developing countries. From 1945 A.D. through 1992 A.D. over 92 percent of all wars were in developing countries.[7]

Since World War II, both developed, developing, and even underdeveloped countries have sought superiority in military power. As of 1993 A.D., developed countries spent as much on military power in a year as the total income of the poorest 2 billion people on earth.[8] Since World War II, global military spending has added up to a cumulative $30–35 trillion.[9] Today, between 5 and 6 percent of the world's total annual product is spent on military affairs.[10] This means that the world spends $1,900,000 each minute for the purpose of war.[11]

It is not just a cliché, but a reality that those who already have, grow rich, while those who have little, see even what they have, taken away. Worse still, it is likely that the distance between the rich and poor will not narrow, but rather continue to widen, to the detriment of the majority, and indeed to the whole of the earth's population. Our world has never seen such economic oppression, unjust economic distribution, and poverty as we have today. According to Fernand Braudel, less than two centuries ago "before the Industrial Revolution, the life standard was almost the same everywhere in the world, approximately $200 a year on the basis of the 1960 A.D. exchange rate, with a slight advantage in favor of the ancient Asiatic civilizations."[12] While two centuries ago the average *per capita* income in the richest countries was just a few times greater than the poorest, today we can see a disparity in some cases of almost one hundred percent between rich and poor. While the Third World nations contain 76 percent of the world's population, they earn only 27 percent of the world's income.[13]

In great part due to this extravagant military spending and uneven economic distribution, over one billion people live in absolute poverty.[14] According to the World Development Report of 1994 A.D., one billion people in developing countries lacked clean water and nearly two billion people lacked adequate sanitation.[15] More than 99 percent of deaths from infectious diseases occur in developing countries, most of which spend much more money for militarization than for health.[16] In addition, millions of adults every year have died of conditions that can be inexpensively prevented or cured.[17] Illiteracy is also a serious problem in developing countries. According to Ruth Leger Sivard, "one-quarter of the adults in the world cannot read and write, and most of them are in the low-income countries. Over half of the adults in South Asia and in Africa are illiterate, and almost half of those in the Middle East as well."[18]

Why are the people who live in developing or underdeveloped countries hungry, illiterate, poor and far from meeting basic human needs? Is it because of a lack of resources, or is it because of a lack of will? The problems of poverty, starvation, poor health, and illiteracy, which prevail in the world today are not due to the lack of resources, but are rather due to the misuse and abuse of resources and unjust wealth distribution. As Renner points out, "If governments pursued the building of a peace system with the same seriousness as they built military muscle, in all likelihood many violent conflicts could be avoided and the problem of health, education, housing, poverty, and environmental sustainability could be solved."[19] He maintains, "A comparatively small investment—perhaps $20–30 billion per year—could make a tremendous difference in the global war and peace balance."[20] However, in 1995 A.D. only $3.36 billion was spent for peacekeeping operations (themselves benefactors of the military/industrial complex), and that was "equivalent to less than half of 1 percent of global military spending."[21]

Can Christians and Muslims together play a role in bringing peace and justice to the world in which we live? Our answer must be both "yes" and "no." As R. C. Johnson points out, "Religion offers no short-term solution, no palliative or panacea for the world's ills likely to find an immediate application. But unquestionably religion offers to men the only final solution of the world's problems, but it is a long-term solution."[22] Focusing on differing theologies of the end, rather than focusing on the common needs of the present, limits our cooperation. Today, religious differences remain one of the most common reasons for wars and conflicts. As George N. Malek points out, "In the Middle East, in particular, and other Islamic lands in general, there can be no peace with the West politically, economically, or otherwise, until resolutions with religious issues are made."[23]

There are limits, but what can be achieved? An answer to this question can be continuing inter-religious dialogue on points of common, human concern. Hans Küng has written, ". . . no world peace without peace among religions, no peace among religions without dialogue between the religions, and no dialogue between the religions without accurate knowledge of one another."[24] I believe in the importance and the necessity of inter-religious dialogue, and there are many reasons for having dialogue between and among the followers of different faiths today. However, we must be sincere and open about our motives. What are Muslims to think of such opportunities for dialogue, when a partner says, "Neither our respect for these religions nor the high esteem in which we hold them nor the complexity of the question involved should deter the Church from proclaiming the message of Jesus Christ to these non-Christians?"[25] As Norman Daniel says, both Muslims and Christians should be honest and sincere about understanding their own religions and their approaches to other religions. He points out:

> Indifference and pragmatism are not a solution. The same basic relationship between the two religions subsists as always. The most irenic of observers must accept that there are irreducible differences between nonnegotiable doctrines. Both sides deceive themselves if they think otherwise. The Christian creeds and the Qur'an are simply incompatible and there is no possibility of reconciling the content of the two faiths, each of which is exclusive, as long as they retain there identities. If either of them does not, the problem is not solved, it is obliterated. Is there any future in further discussion?[26]

Some seek a common theological ground shared by all religions. Although this seems to be a positive approach, in practice it denies the essentially held truth of each faith. John Cobb and Raimundo Panikkar admonish us that we must cease our search for a "universal theory," or a "common source" of religions—or even for "one God" within all religions.[27] We accept that the different religions cannot, ultimately, be apples and oranges (for if they were, how could they, or why should they, speak and work together?); we affirm that the value and the necessity of inter-religious dialogue lies in the fact that there *is* something that ties the religions of the world together. The question remains, what is that thing and how do we work together regarding it?[28]

Ismail al-Faruqi addressed some of the issues limiting dialogue as follows: (1) While Christians regard the Bible as imbued with supreme authority, Muslims regard it as a record of the divine word with which human hands have tampered; (2) while Christians regards God as their "buddy," Muslims exalt God as a being beyond such familiarity; and (3) while Christians regard Jesus as the second person of a triune God, Muslims regard him as one of God's human prophets and messengers. Thus, there are limits to theological dialogue.

Priority should instead be given to living our faiths in the common service of humanity. Muslim-Christian dialogue should seek first to establish mutual understanding of our answers to fundamental ethical questions.[29] Riffat Hassan, a Muslim who participates in many inter-religious activities, says, "My experience of Muslim-Christian-Jewish dialogue has convinced me that it is disastrous to begin any dialogue with a discussion on the concept of God, which many theologians assume to be the natural starting point of any theological dialogue in the framework of monotheistic religious tradition."[30]

What should our attitudes be? Should we give up pursuing this kind of inter-religious relationship, or refocus the content of our discussions? In my opinion, instead of rejecting completely the idea of dialogue or relationship between Christians and Muslims, we can develop a model of human liberation from the evils of this world, a model suitable to both religions. If we begin by accepting each other as we are and leave concerns about eternal salvation to the God that we both agree makes ultimate decisions in this regard, then we can work towards solving our many common problems and the evils which bedevil humanity, such as social and economic injustice, poverty, immorality, war, excessive militarization, violence, the violation of human rights, and environmental problems. If the enemy of my enemy is my friend, then let us make a bond of friendship over our common enemies. If Muslims and Christians take lessons from their past quarrels and hostilities, they can make sincere efforts toward mutual understanding and work together for the preservation and fostering of socio-economic justice, moral life, peace and freedom for all human beings.

ISLAM AND OUR COMMON HUMANITY

In order to understand how Muslims can contribute to the needs of our common humanity, we should examine the concept of revelation in Islam.[31] The central point around which the call of all the prophets revolves is the oneness of God. This teaching, in turn, has always been connected to the socio-economic conditions of the people to whom the prophets were sent. The idea of one almighty God, creator and sustainer of the whole universe, implied the idea of one humanity, a family whose members were equal in the service of God. It can be said that a basic concept of all similarly revealed religions is a strong sense of the brotherhood/sisterhood of human beings and their equal status in the eyes of God. "The idea of brotherhood entailed that they were all responsible for each other's welfare and no individual or group of people could thrive at the expense of others."[32]

In an Islamic understanding, all people in the world are responsible for creating an egalitarian and just moral-social order, but the Muslim community is particularly responsible to God for this function.[33] The Qur'an addresses the Muslim community saying, "Even so we have constituted you as a median community [i.e., between the imperviousness of Judaism and the liquidity of Christianity] that you be witnesses to mankind and that the Messenger be a witness over you (al-Baqara [2]:143)."[34] Muslims were described as "The best community produced for mankind who command good and forbid evil and believe in God (Al 'Imran [3]:104, 110). Enjoining what is right and forbidding what is wrong is one of the main tasks of the Muslim community. The Qur'an says, "(They are) those who, if We establish them in the land, establish regular prayer and give *zakat* (poor tax), enjoin the right and forbid wrong" (al-Hajj [22]:41).

The aim of being an Islamic community is to spread goodness and prevent all kinds of evils.[35] According to the Qur'an, Muslims must protect themselves against injustice. In addition, they have the responsibility to protect the weak from any kind of injustice and oppression. This is the reason for waging war against oppressors.[36] The Qur'an says, "And why should ye not fight in the cause of Allah and of those who, being weak, are ill-treated (and oppressed)?—Men, women, and children, whose cry is: 'Our Lord! Rescue us from this town, whose people are oppressors; and raise for us from thee one who will protect; and raise for us from Thee one who will help!" (al-Nisa [4]:75). The boundaries of Allah could not be transgressed and Muslims were to behave justly towards an enemy. If peace was initiated by the enemy, then Muslims should return that peace.[37] To sum up, eliminating corruption on the earth and reforming the earth is the main concern of the Muslim community.

Social responsibility is a core matter of faith in Islam. According to qur'anic teaching individual piety through worship is not enough for salvation. Without discharging duties towards others, one cannot expect salvation. Prayer alone, the Qur'an says, will not help believers on the Day of Judgment, "Have you seen him who denies the judgment? That is one who repulses the orphan (with harshness). Ah, woe unto worshippers, who are heedless of their prayer; who want but to be seen (at worship), Yet refuse small kindness" (al-Ma'un [107]: 1–7). Those who do not help the needy are seen as those who deny the judgment. The Qur'an asks Muslims to share their wealth with others and says, "You will not attain piety until you spend of that which you love. And whatsoever you spend, Allah is aware thereof" (Al 'Imran [3]:92). Moreover, the Qur'an bestows upon the poor an automatic right to the wealth of the community through the institution of the *zakat* (a wealth tax). Since *zakat,* one of the five pillars of Islam, is placed on the same level as a profession of faith and worship of God through regular prayers, one can argue that the right of the poor to the wealth of the community is an unchallengeable, unquestionable right in Islam. The Qur'an puts it this way, "And in their wealth there is acknowledged right for the needy and destitute" (Al 'Imran [3]:92).

From these verses, it should not be understood that Islam has accepted poverty as a virtue or necessity. On the contrary, poverty has been described as a divine curse, and people are warned against it. Abstinence and self-imposed poverty, therefore, are no virtue in Islam.[38] Two of five pillars in Islam are related to the material conditions, and it is required just of rich Muslims to give *zakat* or go on pilgrimage.

The Qur'an gives a great importance to the pursuit of socio-economic justice. A believer's actions are actually divided into duty towards God and duty towards God's creatures: *Huququllah* and *Huququl-Ibad.* It is said that God may forgive those who fail in performing their duties towards Him, but those who commit sin against their fellow beings will never be forgiven unless the persons concerned forgive them.[39]

Moreover, the Qur'an commands Muslims not to give *only to Muslims* in order to be rewarded on the Day of Judgment. When the Qur'an was being revealed and Muslims were asked to give in the name of God, some people hesitated to give monetary help to non-Muslims, considering it a wasteful investment. To this the Qur'an revealed, "You are not responsible for their guidance; Allah Himself shows guidance to anyone He pleases. Moreover, whatever wealth you spend in charity, it is for your own good. As you spend of your wealth to win Allah's pleasure, you will be given full reward for whatever you spend and you will not be deprived in the least of your rightful due"(al-Baqara [2]:272). Thus, the act of giving, irrespective of the creed of the receiver, is an act of piety in Islam. Islam provides for the economic rights of the poor and disadvantaged. All persons should have access to the necessities of food, clothing, shelter, education and health care, irrespective of their age, sex, color or religion. For those who cannot take care of themselves due to some temporary or permanent disability, it is the obligation of the community to provide social security.[40]

Islam liberates people not only from the fetters of socio-economic bondage, but also from the clutches of those who may control them in the name of religion. The Qur'an always recognizes the existence of other religions. It does not demand that all humanity must embrace Islam. Muslims are not allowed to shove their faith down people's throats. Their duty is only to convey the message of Islam and to leave the rest to God. This was true even for the Prophet himself: the Qur'an consoled him when his message was refused by his own people. It said, "Remind them, for you are but a reminder. You are not at all a warder over them" (al-Ghashiya [88]:21–22). The Qur'an criticizes the Jews and the Christians for their belief that none but people belonging to their group will enter paradise. It rejects that idea as "a dream"; salvation is not confined to any particular group. The Qur'an has set its basic requirement, salvation is only for those who surrender before God and do what is right. Only will such people be rewarded by God and there shall be no fear in them, neither shall they grieve. This means that salvation is a matter exclusively in the hands of God who is well above all prejudices and partisanship.[41]

The task of the Muslim community is not only to perform a few prayers or to worship, but also to establish a society where everyone can accomplish his/her basic human rights irrespective of his/her creed, color, and nationality.

CHRISTIANITY AND OUR COMMON HUMANITY

When we examine the Bible, we can easily see a concern for all humanity. All people are created in the image of God (Gen.1:27); God is the creator of heaven and earth (Gen. 14:19–22; Isa. 40:28; 45:18); creation proclaims God's glory (Ps. 89:6–12), and it is "very good" (Gen. 1:31). At the summit of creation stands the creation of man and woman, made in God's image (Gen. 1:26–27). This implies that no dimension of all of human life lies beyond God's care and concern. "As such every human being possesses an inalienable dignity that stamps human existence prior to any division into races or nations and prior to human labor and human achievement (Gen. 4–11).[42]

The Covenant at Sinai (Ex. 19–24) is deeply imbued with this concern. Specific laws of the covenant protect human life and property, demand respect for parents and the spouses and the children of one's neighbor. They manifest a special concern for the vulnerable members of the community: widows, orphans, the poor, and strangers in the land. "The codes of Israel reflect the norms of the covenant: reciprocal responsibility, mercy, and truth-fulness. They embody a life of freedom from oppression, worship of the One God, rejection of idolatry, mutual respect among people, care and protection for every member of the social body."[43] It is understood from this that being free and being a co-responsible community are God's intentions for believers.

Biblical faith in general, and prophetic faith especially, insists that fidelity to the covenant joins obedience to God with reverence and concern for the neighbor. The biblical terms that summarize this double dimension of Israel's faith are *sedaqah* (justice or righteousness) and *mishpat* (right judgment or justice embodied in a concrete act or deed).[44]

In the Old Testament, God is described as a "God of justice" (Isa. 30:18), one who loves justice (Isa. 61:8, cf. Ps. 11:7; 33:5; 37:28; 99:4) and delights in it (Jer. 9:23). God demands justice from the whole people (Deut. 16:20) and executes justice for the needy (Ps. 140:13). This justice of the Bible is measured by the treatment of the powerless in society, most often described as the widow, the orphan, the poor, and the stranger in the land. The Law, the Prophets, and Wisdom literature of the Old Testament all show deep concern for the proper treatment of such people.[45] What these groups of people have in common is their vulnerability and lack of power. They are often alone and have no protector or advocate. Therefore, the Bible castigates not only the worship of idols, but also manifestations of idolatry, such as the quest for un-restrained power and the desire for great wealth at the expense of others (Isa. 40:12–20; 44:1–20; Wis. 13:1–14:31; Col. 3:5).

The same concern for the poor, needy and vulnerable person is a focus of the New Testament. The first public utterance of Jesus was related to the poor, "The Spirit of the Lord is upon me, therefore he has anointed me. He has sent me to bring glad tidings to the poor" (Lk. 4:18). Jesus takes the side of those most in need. In the Last Judgment, as dramatically described in St. Matthew's Gospel, the followers of Jesus will be judged according to how they respond to the hungry, the thirsty, the naked, and the stranger. As fol-lowers of Christ, they are challenged to make a fundamental "option for the poor"—to speak for the voiceless, to defend the defenseless, to assess lifestyles, policies, and social institutions in terms of their impact on the poor.[46]

Jesus warns against attempts to "lay up treasures on earth" (Mt. 6:19), and exhorts his followers not to be anxious about material goods but rather to seek first God's reign and God's justice (Mt. 6:25–33). When asked what was the greatest commandment, Jesus quoted the old Jewish affirmation of faith that God alone is One and should be loved with the whole heart, mind, and soul (Deut. 6:4–5) and immediately added, "You shall love your neighbor as your-self" (Lev. 19:18, Mk. 12:28–34). Near the end of his life, Jesus offered a vivid picture of the Last Judgment (Mt. 25:31–46). According to this picture, all the nations of the world will be assembled and will be divided into those blessed who are welcomed into God's kingdom or those cursed who are sent to eternal punishment. The blessed are those who fed the hungry, gave drink to the thirsty, welcomed the stranger, clothed the naked, and visited the sick and imprisoned; the cursed are those who neglected these works of mercy and love.

Christian discipleship involves imitating the pattern of Jesus' life in the service of others (Mk. 10:42–45). Jesus, especially in Luke, lives as a poor man, takes the side of the poor, and warns of the dangers of wealth. Throughout the Bible, material poverty is a misfortune and a cause of sadness, yet Jesus gives dignity to those who suffer under it. A constant biblical refrain is that the poor must be cared for and protected and that when they are exploited, God hears their cries (Prv. 22:22–23).[47] Jesus offers himself as the model of all-inclusive love: ". . . love one another as I have loved you" (Jn. 15:12).

One can well ask, the Bible gives great importance to matters of socioeconomic justice, but do Christians in our day show the same concern? I am not in a position to judge. I do know that at least some groups of Christians strive in this regard. I can identify, for example, Catholic Bishops who wrote books on justice and peace.[48] I am challenged by their writing. However, are these the Christians that Muslims know?

> No one may claim the name Christian and be comfortable in the face of hunger, homelessness, insecurity, and injustice found in this country and the world. . . . We seek the cooperation and support of those who do not share our faith or tradition.[49]

For these Bishops, violence has many faces: oppression of the poor, deprivation of basic human rights, economic exploitation, sexual exploitation and pornography, neglect or abuse of the aged and the helpless, and other acts of inhumanity.[50] They add that, "No society can live in peace with itself, or with the world, without a full awareness of the worth and dignity of every human person, and of the sacredness of all human life (Jas. 4:1–2)."[51]

CONCLUDING REMARKS

We live in a more pluralistic world than ages past, and we need each other in every aspect of life. The problems of the world cannot be limited to only one or a few nations, but all nations and their peoples are affected by the concerns of our common humanity. How can Christians and Muslims be a part of the solution rather than a part of the problem?

The first thing that came to mind was the inter-religious dialogue that emerged in the 1960s. We can learn many things from each other through inter-religious dialogue. However, if we see it as a way of converting people to our religion or of granting salvation to others, we will limit what we can do together in meeting the concerns of our common humanity.

This kind of action and thinking is not a matter for just Africans, Asians, Europeans or Latin Americans, but for all. The human need for economic and political justice, and for freedom from (especially nuclear) violence, is too big a job for any one nation, culture, or religion. In order to tackle these big problems, which threaten the whole world, Christians and Muslims need to be involved in worldwide inter-religious cooperation as well as dialogue. The relevance of our religions can be evaluated in terms of their contributions to the solutions of world problems. As Knitter writes, ". . . religion that does not address, as a primary concern, the poverty and oppression that infest our world is not authentic religion."[52]

With such enormous human problems, what is the point of arguing about the uniqueness, finality or the salvific positions of the religions? Right practice (orthopraxy) is at least as important to Muslims and Christians as right knowing (orthodoxy). Both of our scriptures tell us so; yet we do not do what is in our power to address the evils in this world. It is false to think that we can agree on our theologies without rendering meaningless our two faiths, but it is imperative that we are together in the struggle against those things that threaten our globe. This point is stressed in both the Bible and the Qur'an, "not those who proclaim only 'Lord, Lord,' but those who *do* the will of the Father will enter the kingdom (Mt. 7:21–23) and

> Virtue does not mean for you to turn your faces towards the East and West, but virtue means one should believe in God, the Last Day, angels, the Book and prophets; and no matter how he loves it, to give his wealth away to near relatives, orphans, the needy, the wayfarer and beggars, and towards freeing captives; and to keep up prayer and pay the welfare tax; and those who keep their word whenever they promise anything; and are patient under suffering and hardship and in time of violence. Those are the ones who act loyal, and they perform their duty (al-Baqara [2]: 177).

The basic aim of inter-religious dialogue should be to address common human issues, to take a stand together against things that create poverty and harm the dignity of human beings. The Qur'an commands this: "Help ye one another in righteousness and piety, but help ye not one another in sin and rancor: Fear Allah, for Allah is strict in punishment" (al-Ma'ida [5]:2).

NOTES

1. Hans Küng, "Christianity and World Religions: Dialogue with Islam," in *Toward a Universal Theology of Religion*, ed. Leonard Swidler (New York: Orbis Books, 1988), p. 193.

2. Betty A. Reardon, *Militarization, Security, and Peace Education* (Valley Forge, PA.: United Ministries in Education, 1982), p. 39.

3. Quincy Wright, *A Study of War* (Chicago: University of Chicago Press, 1965), p. 626, table 22.

4. Ruth L. Sivard, *World Military and Social Expenditures 1993* (Washington, D.C.: World Priorities, 1993), p. 20.

5. David Krieger and Frank K. Kelly, "Introduction," in *Waging Peace II: Vision and Hope for the 21ˢᵗ Century*, ed. David Krieger and Frank K. Kelly (Chicago: Noble Press, 1992), p. xv.

6. William Eckhardt, "War-Related Deaths Since 3000 BC," *Peace Research* 23, no 1 (February 1991), p. 83.

7. Sivard, p. 20.

8. Ibid., p. 5.

9. Ibid., p. 152.

10. Ibid., pp. 43–50.

11. Annabel Rodda, *Women and the Environment*, Women and World Development Series (London and N.J.: Zed Books, 1991), p. 38.

12. Fernand Braudel, *Capitalism and Material Life, 1400–1800*, trans. Miriam Kochan (New York: Harper and Row, 1973), p. 93.

13. Jerry Folk, *Doing Theology Doing Justice* (Minneapolis: Fortress Press, 1991), p. 31.

14. Ibid., p. 8.

15. *World Development Report 1994* (Oxford and New York, Oxford University Press, 1994), p. 1.

16. Anne E. Platt, "Infectious Diseases Return," in *Vital Signs 1996: The Trends That Are Shaping Our Future*, ed. Linda Starke (New York and London: W. W. Norton, 1996), pp. 130–31.

17. *World Development Report 1993* (Oxford and New York: Oxford University Press, 1993), p. 1.

18. Sivard, p. 31.

19. Michael Renner, "Budgeting for Disarmament" in *State of the World 1995: A World Watch Institute Report on Progress toward a Sustainable Society*, ed. Linda Starke (New York and London: W. W. Norton, 1995), p. 153.

20. Michael Renner, "Peacekeeping Expenditures Level Off," in *Vital Signs 1996: The Trends That Are Shaping Our Future*, ed. Linda Starke (New York and London: W. W. Norton, 1996), pp. 101–103.

21. Ibid. p. 102–103.

22. R. C. Johnson, "The Influence of Religious Teaching as a Factor in Maintaining Peace," in *Paths to Peace: A Study of War Its Causes and Prevention*, ed. Victor H. Wallace (New York: Books for Libraries Press, 1970), p. 349.

23. George N. Malek, "Christian-Muslim Dialogue," *Missiology: An International Review* 15, no.3 (July 1988), p. 285.

24. Küng, p. 194.

25. Evangelii Nuntiandi, 2, in *Inter-religious Dialogue*, pp. 82–83.

26. Norman Daniel, *Islam and the West: The Making of an Image* (Oxford, Oneworld, 1993), pp. 335–36.

27. Paul F. Knitter, "Toward a Liberation Theology of Religions," in *The Myth of Christian Uniqueness*, ed. John Hick and Paul F. Knitter (Maryknoll, New York: Orbis Books, 1994), p. 184.

28. Ibid., pp. 184–85.

29. Ismail Ragi al-Faruqi, "Islam and Christianity: Diatribe or Dialogue," in *Muslims in Dialogue: The Evolution of a Dialogue*, ed. Leonard Swidler (Lewiston: Edwin Mellen Press, 1992), pp. 15–16.

30. Riffat Hassan, "The Basis for a Hindu-Muslim Dialogue and Steps in That Direction from a Muslim Perspective" in *Muslims in Dialogue: The Evolution of a Dialogue*, ed. Leonard Swidler (Lewiston: Edwin Mellen Press, 1992), p. 419.

31. Zafar Ishaq Ansari, "Some Reflections on Islamic Bases for Dialogue with Jews and Christians," *Journal of Ecumenical Studies*, Vol. XIV, no 3 (Summer 1977), p. 434.

32. Mushir ul-Haq, "Liberation and Justice Motifs in Islam," *Religion and Society*, 24–31. Vol 27, no. 2 (June 1980), p. 25.

33. Fazlur Rahman, *Major Themes of the Qur'an* (Chicago: Bibliotheca Islamica, 1980), p. 62.

34. Rahman's translation.

35. See the Al 'Imran [3]:104, 110, 114; al-Tawba [9]: 71, 112.

36. See for broad information on this issue Majid Khadduri, *War and Peace in the Law of Islam* (Baltimore: Johns Hopkins University Press, 1955); Mahmut Shaltut, "Koran and Fighting," in *Jihad in Medieval and Modern Times*, translated by Rudolph Peters (Leiden: E.J. Brill, 1977), pp. 26–86; Muhammad Abu Zahra, *The Concept of War in Islam*, traslated by Muhammad al-Hady and Taha Omar (Cairo: Ministry of Waqf, n. d.).

37. See al-Baqara [2]:190–93; al-Ma'ida [5]:8; al-Anfal [8]:61; al-Hajj [22]: 39–40, 60.

38. Haq, p. 28.

39. Ibid., p. 30.

40. Chandra Muzaffar, *Human Rights and the New World Order* (Penang, Malaysia: Just World Trust, 1993), pp. 34–36.

41. Al-Baqara [2]:111–113; see also al-Baqara [2]:177.

42. National Conference of Catholic Bishops, *Economic Justice for All: Pastoral Letter on Catholic Social Teaching and the U.S. Economy* (Washington D.C.: National Conference of Catholic Bishops, 1986), p. 17.

43. Ibid., p. 20.

44. Ibid., p. 21.

45. See Ex. 22:20–26; Deut. 15: 1–11; Jb. 29:12–17; Ps. 69:34; 72:2, 4, 12–24; 82:3–4; Prv. 14:21, 31; Isa. 3:14–15; 10:2; Jer. 22:16; Zec. 7:9–10.

46. National Conference of Catholic Bishops, *Economic Justice for All,* pp. x-xi.

47. Ibid., pp. 23–27.

48. These books mentioned above are *Economic Justice for All,* and *The Challange of Peace,* which are used as referances in this paper.

49. National Conference of Catholic Bishops, *Economic Justice for All,* p. 13.

50. National Conference of Catholic Bishops, *The Challenge of Peace: God's Promise and Our Response, A Pastoral Letter on War and Peace* (Washington, D. C.: 1983), p. 119.

51. Ibid.

52. Knitter, p. 180.

Chapter Nine

AN ISLAMIC APPROACH TOWARD INTERNATIONAL PEACE

Israfil Balci
Ondokoz Mayis University
Samsun, Turkey

We frequently use these terms in our daily speech: international peace, dialogue and collaboration. In our globalized world, the boundaries between states are disappearing as states begin to depend on each other more and more. On the one hand this dependence has urged the states to enter into relationship with others. On the other hand it has made those relationships more and more complicated. In their relationship with others, a number of factors play a significant role: namely political, economic, cultural, military and religious. In our world, in which religious values are obtaining such an important role, it is an inevitable reality that religion can contribute a great deal to the establishment of world peace, especially the major world religions such as Judaism, Christianity, Islam, Buddhism and Hinduism.

Within the context of the contribution of Islam to world peace, researchers make different evaluations. For example, according to some evaluations (1) Islam is a religion based on the *umma*; (2) In Islam the options for being other than a Muslim are paying *jizya* (tax) or being killed; (3) Islam sees the outside world as a potential enemy. When we look at the Qur'an, however, none of these evaluations emerge from Islam itself, but only from its historical structures. Depending on these unjust evaluations some scholars argue that Muslim states should never establish peaceful relations with non-Muslim states. Khadduri disagrees with this view.[1] Not just Khadduri, but also Abu Suleyman argues, highlighting similar points, that Muslims have serious problems in their dialogical relationships with others.[2] In this article, we examine the general views and approaches of Islam toward the non-Muslim world. Thus, we will examine the attitude of Islam toward international peace and we will discuss Islam's contribution to our globalized world. As a source for this, we will mainly use the Qur'an and Hadith (the sayings and deeds of the Prophet). In addition, we refer to some classical works as well as some modern works of traditional Sunni Islamic thought.

As is well known, the qur'anic verses are divided into two categories: those verses revealed in Mecca and those revealed in Medina. It must be kept in mind that political and social realities play an important role in the history of revelation. For instance, after the migration (hijra) of the Prophet from Mecca to Medina in 622 A.D., social and economic stratification occurred. The revealed qur'anic verses were tailored to the political and social conditions of the community. What we are concerned with here is the attitudes of the qur'anic verses toward the non-Muslim world. By the provenance of this attitude we will certainly be able to understand the principle approaches of Islam towards international peace.

The moderate approaches toward the People of the book (Ahl al-Kitab) are more noticeable in the qur'anic verses of Mecca. For example, the following verses, which were revealed in Mecca, show a sincere approach toward the People of the Book. The Qur'an reads, "If ye realize this not, ask of those who posses the message" (al-Nahl [16]:43; al-Anbiya [21]:7). Other qur'anic verses, for example, the verses in the Meccan suras, call Muslims to behave in a moderated way toward non-Muslims in a time of struggle. In this sura, the Qur'an does not mention the military or political struggle, but instead uses a soft style of address. The sura of al-Furqan, which was also revealed in Mecca, encouraged Muslims not to submit easily toward non-Muslims, but to make a psychological holy war against them.[3] Consequently, when we examine these verses, we see that the military struggle against the non-Muslim is not mentioned.[4]

The continuation of the moderate attitude toward the People of the Book in the first years of the period of Medina is not a coincidence. Al-'Ankabut, which was revealed in the period of Medina, recommended that Muslims interact kindly with the People of the Book.[5] The Qur'an says:

> And dispute ye not with the People of the Book, excepting in the best way, unless it be with those of them who do wrong but say, We believe in the revelation which has come down to us and in that which came down to you; our God and your God is one, and it is to Him we submit (in Islam). And thus (it is) that we have sent down the Book to thee. So the People of the Book believe therein (al-'Ankabut [29]:46–47).

When we examine the sayings and activities of the Prophet Muhammad, we see that at the beginning, he behaved in a very friendly way toward the

People of the Book. Abu Hurayrah (d. 58 A.H./678 A.D.), one of the narrators of the Hadith, says that, "The Prophet talked about the People of the Book as follows: People of the Book read the Torah in Hebrew, but they explained it in Arabic to the Muslims. Upon this the Prophet said Muslims you should neither approve nor disapprove of their positions, but you should say that we only believed that which was revealed to us and to you, and the God, ours and yours, is one and we all submitted to him."[6]

These examples show us that at the beginning of the period of Medina neither the Prophet nor the Qur'an were against the People of the Book, but they had a neutral attitude toward them. They were accepted as nearer than polytheists for, while Christians had a sacred book, the Arab polytheists associated God with idols. Through this attitude, the Qur'an wanted the People of the Book to come to an agreement with the Muslims in the belief of Allah. This attitude appears in the behavior of the Prophet when he took the side of the Romans against the Zoroastrian Persians in the war between them,[7] and this event is also mentioned in the Qur'an.[8]

In addition, there were some friendly relationships between the Muslims and Christians of Ethiopia, and these relationships continued later. Accordingly, there are a few loyal and respectable letters between the Prophet and the king of Ethiopia. As an expression of this loyalty the Prophet told Muslims "not to attack them unless they attack you."[9] We understand that this loyalty of the Prophet includes all the Ethiopians. This loyalty manifested itself in the leniency of the Prophet toward the Christians of Najran, for the Prophet allowed them to pray in their own way even in the mosques of the Muslims.[10]

After he went to Medina, the Prophet built a socio-cultural and political order, and the Jews, Christians and the polytheists of Medina participated in this order. In this period we see that the Prophet continued with the same concern for the different groups of Medina. From this kind of behavior we can conclude that the Muslims of different ages can agree with the non-Muslims on the issue of peace, charity and prosperity in the world.[11]

There is a gradual increase in hardness of attitude toward the People of the Book from the beginning of the period of Medina to the later years. The reason for this harding can be found in the collaboration of the People of the Book with the enemies of Muslims.[12] The insistence of the People of the Book on this attitude is the main reason for the sharp content of some qur'anic verses.[13] They, however, were not completely excluded, and were treated in accordance with their attitude toward the agreements.[14]

It seems that there are serious contradictions between the verses of the Qur'an and their application in the daily life of traditional Muslims. The main reason for this contradiction is related to the verse dealing with war in the time of peace.[15] This difficulty resulted because of the appearance that the

People of the Book must be humiliated before the Muslims, so the People of the Book were regarded as potential enemies to Muslims. But this understanding, as we noted above, should not be the final and universal rule of the Qur'an.

It appears that the political and social conditions of the traditional Islamic understanding began to change after the war of Tabuk (631 A.D.). The sura of al-Tauba began to be revealed during the preparation for the war of Tabuk. This sura, which was revealed during the war, contains hard statements against the People of the Book. When we look at the situation in terms of wartime conditions, this approach should be accepted as normal. However, what is important for us to note are the different situations between the hot war and the cold war. The qur'anic verses that were revealed during the hot war conditions must not be understood as for cold war conditions. We must consider the context in which these verses were revealed before we interpret them as a general qur'anic attitude toward non-Muslims.[16]

Not to accept the verses of al-Tauba in their historical conditions and instead accept them as a reflection of the universal point of view of Islam is a kind of reductionist approach to Islam because this approach does not reflect the whole of Islam. Traditional commentators on the Qur'an understood the verses of al-Tauba in a literal sense, "but when the forbidden months are past, then fight and slay the pagans wherever ye find them . . ." (9:5). They tried to give a universal rule to these verses, but when they got in trouble in explaining their meaning, they used the traditional doctrine of abrogation (*nesh*) as a solution.[17] By doing this, they did not consider the conditions of that period and the limited meaning of these verses to conflicts confronting the Prophet in Medina. Consequently, when we examine these verses, we must take into consideration the political, social, and military conditions of that time and of the time in which we live.

After the forbidden month (*al-ashhuru'l-hurumu*),[18] some commentators insisted on the impossibility of agreement with non-believers even in normal conditions.[19] Some others concluded that this verse abrogated the verses indicating tolerance toward the non-Muslims to the particular time of tolerance towards the non-Muslims.[20] One of them, for example, is Ibnu 'l-Arabi (d. 543 A.H./1148 A.D.) a Maliki lawyer, who suggested that this verse abrogated 114 verses of the Qur'an.[21] Another scholar, al-Qurtubi (d. 671 A.H./1273 A.D.), quoted the following view from Husayn b. Fadlan that "this verse abrogated all of the verses of the Qur'an enjoining patience and leniency toward the enemies."[22]

It is very interesting that some commentators who hold to the doctrine of abrogation pertinently tried to abolish some verses of the Qur'an that express dialog and agreement with non-Muslims. We should notice that the basis of this understanding is routed in the tension between the Muslim and non-Muslim world. The tension that appeared in the works of these commentators reflects their psychological situations, and this must be accepted as a normal continuation of their style of commentary. This understanding of abrogation is their own particular approach and should not be made to apply to everyone.[23] For example, the philosopher Averroës (d. 595 A.H./1200 A.D) criticizes the traditional theological scholars who hold to the doctrine of abrogation.[24]

According to the Qur'an, every human being is free to choose whatever way he or she wants, and this wholly depends on his or her free will and beliefs.[25] On this matter, there are many verses. To neglect these verses and to force non-believers to believe as Muslims do does not reflect a common Islamic point of view on this topic.[26] Almost all traditional authors presented foreigners with two choices—either war or paying *jizya*, but not a third choice—living in peace.[27]

This general understanding of the Islamic view gradually became a tenet of belief for Muslims and one of the basic foundations of Islamic state-law. The thoughts of al-Saybani, the oldest and most prominent Hanafi lawyer of state-law, are accepted as the general and final attitude of Islamic thought.[28] According to al-Saybani, Muslims cannot accept non-Muslims in the state unless they pay tribute and accept the supremacy of Islam. However, Muslims should accept this agreement only in their weak conditions; when they are strong that agreement should be abolished.[29]

In their lack of understanding of the real aim of the Qur'an, such traditional scholars divided the world in two artificial spheres: *dar al-Islam (house of Islam)* and *dar al-harb (house of war)*.[30] This division appears in the structure of medieval Islamic states.[31] In other words, the tolerant and moderate approaches of the Qur'an were lost. In the following verses the Qur'an indicates that Muslim should establish peaceful relationships with others:

But when ye are clear of the sacred precincts and of pilgrim garb, ye may hunt and let not the hatred of some people, in (once) shutting you out of the sacred Mosque lead you to transgression (and hostility on your part). Help ye not one another in sin and rancor . . . (al-Ma'ida [5]:2).

Allah forbids you not, from dealing kindly and justly with those who do not fight for (your) faith nor drive you out of your homes. For Allah loveth those who are just. Allah only forbids you from turning (for friendship and protection) to those who fight you for (your) faith, and drive you out of your homes, and support (others) in driving you out. It is such as turn to them (in these circumstances) that do wrong (al-Mumtahana [60]:8–9).

Christian scholars also divided the world into two spheres in the medieval age, as did Muslims: the world of Christianity and the world of idolatry. Foreigners in the western world were often considered barbarians, because the western world was affected by ancient Greek and Roman thought. However, we will not discuss the situations and problems of the medieval age. This is not our concern here. Our concern is how religions, whose roots are peace, justice, tolerance, and compassion, can make a positive contribution to world peace. Our world needs more of this kind of dialogue. The qur'anic verses and many examples in the history of Islam show that dialogue is rooted in Islam.

NOTES

1. Majid Khadduri, *War and Peace in the Law of Islam* (Baltimore: The John Hopkins Press, 1955), p. 44.
2. Ahmad Abu Suleyman, *Islam in Uluslararasi ilikiler Kurami*, translated Fehmi Koru (Istanbul, 1985), p. 10.
3. Al-Furqan, [25]:52.
4. Bassam Tibi, "War and Peace in Islamic Law," *The Ethics of War and Peace Religious and Secular Perspectives*, (Princeton: Princeton University Press, 1996), p.132.
5. Abulfarac Camaludin Abdurrahmdn b. Ali al–Cevzi (597 A.H/1201 A.D.), *Zad al-Masir fi 'Ilm at-Tafsir* (Beirut), VI, 253; Mehmet Okuyan-Mustafa Ozturk, "Kur'an Verilerine Gore Otekinin Konumu," *Islam ve Oteki*, ed. Cafer Sadik Yaran (Istanbul, 2001), pp. 177–78.
6. Ibn al-Cavzi, VI, 276.
7. Abu al-Rasan Ali b. Ahmad al–Vahidi, *Asbftb an-Nuzul* (Cairo, 1388/1968), pp. 231–32.
8. Al-Rum [30]:3–4.
9. Abu Dawud (d. 275/288–89), *Sunan* (Hims, 1969), Malahim, 31/8.
10. Abu Abdillah Muhammad b. Sa'd (d. 230 A.H/845 A.D.), *al- Tabaqat al-Kubra* (Beirut: Dar al-Fikr, undated), I, 358–59; Muhammad Hamidullah, *Foreign Relations of the Prophet With the Countries of Middle-East, India, and China* (Hydarabad, 1985), p. 15; Afzal Iqbal, *The Prophet's Diplomacy* (Delhi: C. Stark, 1984), pp. 60–61; A Rldvan Ahmad, *al-Astal, Vuftidu fi Ahdi al-Makki wa Asaruha al-'I'lami* (Jordan: al-Zurqa, 1404/1984), pp. 128–29.
11. Averros (1200/595), *Bidaya al-Mujtahid wa Nihaya al-Muqtasid*, ed. A Muhammad Abdulhalim-Abdurrahman Husayn Muhamad (Cairo undated), 1,412; W M. Watt, *Islam Nedir*, translated ElifRlza, second ed. (Istanbul, 1993), p. 107.
12. Al 'Imran [3]:65, 71, 98, 99.
13. Al-Baqara [2]:79, 63–64, 87, 97, 100, 109, 146, 211, 213; Al 'Imran [3]:23, 65, 70–71, 99, 100, 110, 185; al-Nisa [4]:17, 44, 46, 51, 155; al-Ma'ida [5]:13, 18, 41, 57, 77, 80–81; al-Tawba [9]:30–31.

14. Al 'Imran [3]:199, 110; al-Nisa [4]:162.

15. Al-Baqara [2]:63–64, 87, 100, 109, 146; Al 'Imran [3]:70–71, 110; al-Nisa [4]:44, 155; al-Mai'da [5]:81.

16. Muhammad Asad, *Kur'an Mesajl: Meal-Tefsir*, translated by Cahit Koytak-Ahmet Erturk (Istanbul, 1996), pp. 1,343.

17. Averroës, 1,415–16; Abu Suleyman, p. 41.

18. During this time, the war was forbidden for Muslims.

19. Abu Ca'far Muhammad b. Jarir At- Tabari (d. 310 A.H./992 A.D.), *al-Cami' al-Bayan 'An Ta'vili Ayi al-Qur'an* (Beirut, 1988), X, 78– 79; Nasr b. Muhammad b. Ahmad Abu'I-Lays al-Samarkandi, *al-Bahr al-Ulum* (Beirut, 1996), II, 40; Abu Bakr Ahmad b. Razi al-Cassas (d. 370 A.H./980 A.D.), *Ahkam al-Qur'an*,ed. Muhammad Sadlk Kamhavi (Beirut, n.d.), VIII, 47; Ibn Kathir, *at-Tafsir al-Qur'an al-'Azim* (Istanbul, 1984), II, 336.

20. Badruddin Muhammad b. Abdillah al-Zarkasi, *al-Burhan fi 'Ulumi al-Qur'an*, ed Muhammad Abulfadl Abraham (Beirut, n.d.), II, 40–41; Ebu Muhammad Huseyin b. Mes'ud al-Bagavi, *al-Me'alim at-Tanzil*, ed., Halid Abdurrahman al-' Akk-Mervan Suvar (Beirut, 1995), II, 269; Abu Abdillah b. Muhammad b. Ahmad al-Kurtubi (d. 671/1273), *al-Cami' li Ahkam al-Qur'an* (Cairo, 1386–87/1966–67), VIII, 47.

21. Al-Zarkasi, II, 40–41; al-Bagavi, II, 269.

22. Al–Kurtubi, VIII, 47; Okuyan-Ozturk, p. 190.

23. Okuyan-Ozturk, pp. 186–87.

24. Averroës, 1,415–16.

25. Al-Baqara [2]:81–82, 256, 281, 286; al-Nisa [4]:170; al-Tawba [9]:82; Yunus [10]:99, 100, 108; al-Ra'd [13]:29; al-Isra [17]:15; al-Furqan [25]:62; al-Naml [27]:92; al-Mala'ika [35]:18; al-Zumar [39]:41; Fussilat [41]:46; al-Ahqaf [46]:13; al-Najm [53]:37–40; al-Muddaththir [74]:38, 54–55; al-Insan [76]:2–3; 'Abasa [80]:11–12; al-Takwir [81]:27–28; al-Shams [91]:9–10.

26. Ibnu Kayyim al-Cavziyya, pp. 1–7.

27. Ibnu Kayyim al-Cavziyya, 1,23–25; Averroës, 1,328; Ibnu Kudama, (d. 620 A.H./1223 A.D.), *al-Mugni* (Beirut, 1972/1392), IX, 285–89; Abu Abdillfih Muhammad b. Idris al-Safii (d. 240 A.H./819 A.D.), *al-Umm* (Beirut, 1973), IV, 110–112; Hans Kruse, "Islam Devletler Hukukunun Ortaya Cikisi," translated by Yusuf Ziya Kavakc in *Islam Tetkikleri Dergisi*, c. 4, vol. 3– 4 (Istanbul, 1971), pp. 57–70; Khadduri, pp.62–65, pp.176–77; Tibi, pp.131–135.

28. Samsuddin Muhammad b. Ahmad as-Sarahsi, (d. 483 A.H./1090 A.D.), *Sarhu Kitab as-Siyar al-Kabir li-Muhammad b. Hasan as-Saybani*, ed. Salahuddin Munajjid and 'Aziz Ahmad, *Matbfia as-Sirkah al-'l'lanfit* (Cairo, 1971– 72), pp. 187–90.

29. Al-Sarahsi, I, pp. 190–91.

30. Khaddduri, 64–65; Tibi, pp. 131–32.

31. Ebu Suleyman, p. 45.

Chapter Ten

Hegemonic Power Versus *tawhīd*: A Decisive Concept of Islam on Interfaith Relations

Sinasi Gündüz,
Assistant Professor, History of Religions
Ondokoz Mayis University

As Ninian Smart stated, religion has been a vital and pervasive characteristic of human life throughout history. To understand human life and history it is therefore essential to understand religion.[1] We can also mention another important factor that has been at least as effective in human history as religious beliefs: "power" based upon the hegemonic authority. Hence, to better understand human history and life it is also necessary to take into account and examine the factor of hegemonic power which has always been influential.

THE INFLUENCE OF POWER AND IDEOLOGICAL PARADIGMS UPON THE UNDERSTANDING OF RELIGION

"Power" has always been an important part of human life throughout history. It is one of the basic essentials for relations between humans. It was also the most important, although not the only component in the social formation of societies—friends and enemies, decisions of peace and war, pro- or anti-scientific attitudes – in short, in almost every facet of social formation. *Power* has also been considerably effective both in controversies within religion itself and in inter-religious relations. For example, in Middle Age Europe, Catholicism with its anti-scientific attitude carried out a war against civil rights and liberties that caused feelings of anti-religious values to develop and accelerate. This war was caused by the political power that the Papacy held and tried to preserve, rather than by theological reasons proceeding from the religion itself.

The same is also true for some events in Islamic history. For instance, the main reason for dispute and controversy between *ahl al-sunnah* and *shī'ah*, and between Ash'arites and Mutazilah was political rather than theological. Even the theological arguments held by the parties were coloured by political motivations, because dynasties such as the Umayyads or Abbasids generally adopted a theological position as an official point of view and desired people under their authority to accept it. Consequently, from time to time, they forced those under their authority to accept certain politically motivated theologies. For instance, this can be seen at the time of the Abbāsid caliph al-Ma'mun who instituted *al-mihnah* to persecute those who did not accept Mutazilate views. We can see the same in the case of the Crusades, which left deep and bitter memories in history. Although it is true that some reasons connected with religious sentiments, such as rescuing the holy land from the infidels, re-establishing the security of the pilgrimage routes and so on were used for the Crusades, the most prominent reason for these campaigns, it would appear, was to defend the power and political authority held by the Papacy and Christian, Western kingships. The Crusades were a reaction against the new opposing power that had risen in the east and was quickly spreading towards the west.

It is hard to disagree with the conviction held by some writers that religions have not historically caused peace, but strife and warfare, and that religions with such features as jihad, the Inquisition or the Crusades have an imperialistic character.[2] Similarly, it is unlikely that the war between Iran and Iraq, the enmity between India and Pakistan or the conflict in the Middle East are primarily based on religious enmity.[3] As mentioned above, it is true that some terrible events in history between Muslims and Christians and between the followers of various other religions were experienced and are still being experienced. Again, it is true that religious differences are a contributing factor to these terrible events. However, when these events are carefully examined it is obvious that the major reasons behind these conflicts concern the struggle for socio-political power rather than the religious differences. Likewise, it is evident that the major reasons for the bloody conflicts and battles in the Middle East, the Balkans, Caucuses, Indonesia, Ethiopia and Northern Ireland going on today are the socio-political struggles and orientations based upon various internal and external factors related to hegemonic power.

The Church, which was the main force in Europe during the Middle Ages, held the socio-political power to a great extent under its control. The unwilling attitude of the Church to share the power it held with the secular circles and its taking a position against science and freedom of thought laid the groundwork for the formation of major opposition against the Church. So, there came into being an important reaction against the Church and its values, and against the traditional authorities in cooperation with the Church. Thus, with the French Revolution in the 18th century, during which both religious and traditional authorities were questioned and shaken, "power" changed hands and reshaped the West. The religious authority represented by the Pope (and some traditional kingships/authorities) left the power, though unwillingly, to the new socio-political movements that were generally against the Church. Consequently the Church and political power were separated in many western countries. As E. Mortimer rightly stressed,[4] the Church, which was forced to leave the worldly authority to the civil/secular forces, returned to its original doctrines.

Correspondingly, new ideological outlooks and paradigms, which were later effective in shaping the socio-cultural and political construction of the western societies, were shaped according to the new forces. In this period, generally known as the Enlightenment, the new actors of socio-cultural life were mainly the secular forces. They filled the area left by the religious authority with ideologies and paradigms directly or indirectly associated with secularity. Here, I am not necessarily talking about a one-way connection—arguing that either the political forces determined the ideological paradigms or *vice versa*. Rather, these two factors, namely political forces and ideologies/paradigms, are reciprocal influences and assist each other in development.

This new power and ideological process has been effective in the formation and constitution of various scientific disciplines and in the understanding of science. For example, the "scientific method" which endeavors to restrict scientific knowledge to reason and experimental data (empiricism) appeared as a result. Again, the rise "positivism" as the new religion of humanity, after mythological and metaphysical periods, was the product of this period and its anti-religious feelings. This new position was, of course, the fierce response of western society and intellectual circles who, distressed by the despotism and oppression of the Church, enjoyed the new socio-political situation that stressed more liberty. Against the previous ecclesio-centric character of religious authority, the core of the new paradigm was humanistic with such human values as reason and aesthetics. This paradigm was influential until the second half of the 20th century when, especially after World War II, there appeared criticism of this paradigm and the ideologies related to it.

What I want to say here is that the prevalent socio-cultural discourses, motivations and attitudes are not free from the influence of the hegemonic power and ideological paradigms connected with power. In fact, these discourses and attitudes are usually largely determined and directed by power and ideological paradigms.

PLURALISTIC EVALUATION OF RELIGIOUS TRUTH /
REALITY AND HEGEMONIC POWER

During the last century, there has been a remarkable change in discourse regarding both the understanding of religion and inter-religious relations. Scholars of the so-called Enlightenment have generally defined religion and religious matters from a positivistic point of view. Some have even described religion as "the opium of the people." From the second half of the last century onwards, pluralistic evaluations of religion have appeared with especially noticeable discourse about the historical appearance of religion and the truth/reality claims of religious traditions.[5] It seems that the factors of hegemonic power and ideological paradigms were also influential in the pluralistic points of view, since pluralistic views basically move from (and refer to) social and political data rather than religious data. In pluralistic views, where reality, salvation, ethics and relations with others are concerned, what is referred to first is not religion itself but such paradigms as globalization (or the world's current situation of 'global villageness'), secularism, humanism, unity of humanity and society, and current political problems. In fact, pluralism is itself a paradigm of the current era. Pluralistic views, therefore, try to explain religion and religious concepts according to these paradigms.[6] It seems obvious that the basic aim of pluralistic approaches is not phenomenological understanding but the ideological directing of religion and religious sources.

It is, of course, not the purpose of this study to examine pluralism or the pluralistic understanding of religion and inter-religious relations. What I want to stress is that the pluralistic theories concerning religion and religious concepts, including one's attitude toward the other(s), do not originate primarily from within religion but are largely determined by hegemonic powers and ideological paradigms.

Conversely, if we talk about religion and religious concepts such as salvation, truth and reality, we have first of all to take into consideration religion itself and not merely the current ideological paradigms. What I mean by "religion" is the basic sources of a religion like their scripture and historical experience. Secondly, where the relationship of one religion to another is concerned, we have to rely on the religion concerned and analyse its position without causing any assimilation of its structure or ignoring (or changing) its characteristic features. For it is quite important not to pervert the religious concepts and notions and not to impair the religious beliefs, because a religion which is interpreted or impaired according to the perspectives of current socio-political conditions and ideologies/paradigms will be far removed from its essential position, and the new understanding that appears will simply be a heretical (or heterodoxal) version of that religion.

I briefly want to mention some views on the understanding of reality and salvation in religions. Pluralist theories on this subject argue that reality and salvation are not exclusively restricted to any religious tradition since, according to these theories, every religion may lead its followers to reality and salvation. Some of the pluralist thinkers give the famous parable of "the blind men and the elephant" as an example to explain the relation of religions with reality. In this analogy, it is quite interesting that while the elephant represents reality, and the blind men represent the religious traditions, the pluralist himself/herself represents, though indirectly, the king who put the elephant and the blind men into a room, and who sees or realizes the elephant as a whole. This is the key point in showing the fundamental mentality of a pluralistic understanding of religion.

Pluralistic views also hold the idea that religions should not be in a position of defending that they are the only true (unique) way of salvation and that others are wrong. Religions should not espouse that they are the absolute reality and that final salvation belongs exclusively to them. Pluralistic theories argue that unless religions change their traditional, exclusivist position against other religions or see their understanding of reality/salvation as decisive, a sound inter-religious relation or dialogue becomes impossible.[7] Yet, every religious system (most of all Islam, Christianity and other universal religions) presents its followers with an understanding of a unique reality and truth by which alone salvation is possible. The believers stick firm to their religious beliefs and cults with these understandings of absolute reality and salvation. By arguing for the idea that reality or truth, and hence salvation, are not restricted to any particular religion, the pluralistic approach is contrary to the understanding of religion itself (for example the understanding of Islam which presents Islam as the only absolute way of Allah, or Christianity which holds salvation is only through the Messiah, and Mandaeanism which explains the reality with a dualistic belief in God and with an antagonism of spirit and body). With its understanding of reality and salvation the pluralistic approach also weakens the ties between religion and believers, and, hence, damages the individual's piety.

Here this question should be answered: Is the absolute truth claim of religions an obstacle for sound inter-religious relations based upon mutual trust and understanding? The pluralist approach thinks it is, but I disagree for various reasons. First of all, absolute truth or salvation claim of a religion does not require one to see the other(s) as an enemy or to be disrespectful of the other(s). Reality / truth and salvation as religious doctrines are basically concerned with the metaphysical world and oriented towards metaphysical aims. For instance in theist traditions, salvation or truth in a religious sense, is a relation between man and deity (or deities). In this context, the situation of a person or persons who are outside of religious reality and salvation is a problem that should be mainly discussed from the point of divine attributes such as justice, might, willing, judgment and so on. In the same way, from the theistic point of view, God / gods and heavenly beings (or worlds) have the ultimate power to judge and decide who really reached salvation and absolute reality and who did not. Religion, in other words, only shows what the way of salvation and reality is and how to achieve it, but the judgment and decision belong to God. Therefore, it does not mean that having different understandings of reality and salvation in different religions or having absolute truth claims in every religion necessitates enmity between followers of the various religions in social, cultural and political milieus.

Another point, which should be discussed here is the ideological paradigm of globalization, which is connected with the current hegemonic power that seems to lessen the diversity of humanity and almost envisages homogeneity. It is unfortunate that the pluralistic approach with its understanding of religious reality/truth and its understanding of religions' historical mission as different human answers to the same reality is in accord with this ideological paradigm. On the other hand, various belief systems that gather their adherents around the idea of absolute truth are an expression of the cultural richness of humanity and of living together with variety and diversity, since throughout history religions have reflected the plurality of truth and every religion has represented its own understanding. So the religious traditions with their differences contribute much to the cultural richness of humanity. In order to preserve and perpetuate this richness, adherents of different religions should live together (though they may argue with each other on various subjects including reality and salvation) without modifying their religious concepts and discourses due to the pressure of the hegemonic powers and ideologies.

Tawhīd, an important concept of Islamic thought, is a point of understanding, proposed by Islam. *Tawhīd* throughout Islamic history has resisted the hegemonic powers that try to hold humanity's free will and religious preferences under their dominance. *Tawhīd*, as an expression of the unity and uniqueness of God and reality and as an expression of the centrality of God in human life, has always been a guide for the Islamic understanding of inter-human and interfaith relations, as well as an understanding of humanity and the world. *Tawhīd* also has been a guide for believers from the beginning of history against the changing situations since, according to the Qur'an, Islamic history comprises all of humanity from the beginning of time to the very end.

TAWHĪD: ISLAMIC DOCTRINE OF TRUTH/REALITY

Comprised of millions of people throughout the world, Islam is the youngest of the large universal religions. The Qur'an maintains that Islam is the only true religion of God and that no religion other than Islam is accepted by Allah.[8] Since Islam is the only religion of Allah, it is unlawful for a person to desire or to incline to others than Him. For, "everyone in the heavens and on earth has submitted to Him willingly or unwillingly."[9] Islam, which is the expression of submission to Allah, has been preached and represented not only by Muhammad but also by all prophets throughout human history. Abraham, for instance, was a Muslim, and so were his descendants. They declared their submission to God and proclaimed Islam.[10]

Yet, the Qur'an accepts the reality of religions other than Islam and when it talks about them, it explains their existence through such attributes of God as all-willing, all-knowing, just and omnipotent. In the verses of the Qur'an, it is often mentioned that the variety among humanity and the plural structures of human societies and cultures are within the knowledge of God, who permitted humanity to choose their way and tolerated the existence of different ways/religions, though he explained right and wrong and instructed humanity in his true religion from the beginning.[11] Also the Qur'an, from time to time, warns Muhammad and the believers on this subject.[12] All of these examples show that, according to Islam, Allah let the varieties and different ways of humanity exist. Had he wished he would have gathered all humanity in a single nation or in a single way, hindered the unbelieving and unlawful ways, and directed all to the same community. However, he did not wish this because he does not force humans whom he created as *khalīfah*, a different being from the rest of the creatures, who can use their minds and choose freely both right and wrong. However, Allah instructed humanity in what was true and false or *haqq* and *bātil* and wanted them to choose freely their way. Because of this free will humans are responsible for what they have done. This is a necessity of God's justice.

So the Qur'an sometimes reminds Muhammad that to force people to believe is not his business. In fact, he was also told that he has no right or obligation to do this.[13] There is no compulsion in religion; everybody is free in his preference, but whoever has done the least of good he/she will find it and whoever has done the least of evil he/she, again, will find it.[14] It is only Allah, and not anyone else, who will judge humanity. Neither the Prophet nor the believers can judge a human's preference in belief. The duty of the Prophet is only to warn people and to instruct them of what Allah revealed through the Qur'an. Of course, the Qur'an does not leave in doubt what is right and wrong; it clearly explains them and states that whoever seeks wrong beliefs and deeds, after truth/right has been explained clearly, will never be accepted by Allah.[15]

It is also noticeable that in spite of its fierce opposition to disbelief in the true religion of Allah, the Qur'an, in general, has a positive attitude toward some believing systems. The most impressive verse in the Qur'an concerning this is as follows:

> Had Allah not repelled some people by others, surely monasteries (*sawāmi'*), churches (*biya'un*), synagogues (*salawātun*) and mosques (*mesājid*), wherein the name of Allah is mentioned frequently, would have been demolished. Indeed, Allah will support whoever supports Him.[16]

It is noticeable that the Qur'an mentions here monasteries, churches and synagogues together with the mosques as places to be respected for their function. Again the Qur'an never takes the non-believers into consideration as a whole, and never excludes them all. It frequently lays emphasis on the various differences between them. For example, it sometimes compares different believing systems, like Christianity and Judaism, to each other and sometimes stresses varieties within a single religious population. The Qur'an therefore takes into consideration ethical and cultic varieties and distinct attitudes of non-Muslims, and states that they are not all the same.[17]

The Qur'an discusses an important idea when it speaks of reality/truth or salvation, and talks about the historical conflict between right and wrong. This important idea, which is predominant in the arguments of the Qur'an is *tawhīd*; a principle of absolute monotheism which expresses God's centrality in human life and his supreme authority over everything. *Tawhīd* is the most important characteristic of Islamic thought. That is why the Qur'an always uses it as a criterion.[18] In its debate with the followers of other believing systems the Qur'an argues according to the principle of *tawhīd*; when it criticizes some of their beliefs or attitudes, it again refers to *tawhīd*. In short, the principle of *tawhīd* is the basic theme or paradigm of the Qur'an.

Although the term *tawhīd* does not appear in the Qur'an, it is thought that the qur'anic verses, which emphasize Allah's absolute oneness, unity, and superiority, and refuse any associate with him, embody the concept. This concept has consequently been regarded as "the essence of Islam" in Islamic culture, as the famous Muslim scholar Ismail R. Faruki rightly stated. Because of its essential nature in Islamic thought, *'ilm al-tawhīd* has developed in Islamic culture as a scholarly discipline which incorporates other branches of knowledge such as logic, theory of knowledge, metaphysics and ethics.[19]

From another point of view it may seem that the term *tawhīd* refers to theocentrism based upon Allah's centrality. However, one must bear in mind that this is different from theocentrism in the general sense as understood among Western intelligentsia. Theocentrism indicates any god-centered religious tradition, either monotheist or polytheist. Theocentrism in an Islamic sense, however, means Allah's centrality to all of life in the context of *tawhīd*, and expresses not only Allah's unity and oneness in a theological context, but also his centrality in every aspect of human life from individual behaviours to social life and from beliefs to art and aesthetics. In my opinion, it is therefore better to describe Islam as "a tawhīd-centric religion" rather than theocentric.

According to the Qur'an one of the most important features of Islamic thought is this: Allah is the only *ilāh* (God), and there is no other *ilāh* besides him. Because of its importance this expression is the first part of Islamic *shahādah* (declaration of faith). This expression of faith declares that there is no supreme power but Allah, not only in a metaphysical context but in every aspect since the term *ilāh* in Qur'anic usage designates any power who (or which) controls and determines life. Hence, the Qur'an condemns those who use their individual benefits and self-interests as criteria for living their lives, since in turn these powers control them, saying "do you see him who has taken his fancy as his god (*ilāh*)."[20] Again the Qur'an does not restrict the term *ibādah* to only systematic rituals or sacraments (of which examples are seen in every religious tradition), but uses it in the meaning of worship and servitude to God who covers all of one's manners and attitudes. According to the Qur'an the reason humans were created was to worship Allah; therefore, worshipping should permeate the entire life of a human.[21]

Islam describes *tawhīd* as a universal understanding of God beyond history and covering the whole of humanity. It is therefore not restricted to only Muslims who lived during or after the qur'anic period. Hence, the Qur'an examines history from the beginning of time to the very end as a scene of struggle between truth and falsehood or between those who follow the doctrine of *tawhīd* and those who uphold the hegemonic powers. For example, all prophets, according to the Qur'an, instruct their communities in the same principles, which form the doctrine of *tawhīd* as the basic characteristics of Islam. These principles are (1) to accept Allah as the only *ilāh*, (2) to worship him only, and (3) not to associate anybody or anything with him. When the Qur'an speaks of the messages of various prophets, it mentions these fundamental principles.[22] The Qur'an also states that Allah has certainly sent forth messengers to every community in order to teach them the doctrine of *tawhīd* and warn them against disbelief and wrongdoing.[23] So, these messengers have instructed their people about accepting Allah as the only supreme power, worshipping him only and refusing to associate any with him. This is the universal doctrine of truth/reality explained in the Qur'an for which all humans are responsible in the present, future, as well as in the past.

Moreover *tawhīd* is also an expression of God's supreme authority and uniqueness in the context of the relationship between God and the universe and between God and humans. Accordingly, the Qur'an emphasizes that there is no other *ilāh* in heaven and earth; otherwise, both heaven and earth would have been demolished.[24]

Being a universal doctrine of truth/reality that was instructed by the messengers to humanity throughout history, the Islamic doctrine of *tawhīd* suggests that there is (or should be) a unity in reality and, hence, this unity is the source of reality, since Allah is the only (and only source of) reality.[25] So, giving various examples from Noah, Abraham, Moses or Jesus, the Qur'an reminds humanity of this unique reality, which they are responsible to hold and calls humans, in whatever believing system they belong, to accept this truth and follow it.

When the Qur'an talks about non-Muslims and other religious traditions, it takes the doctrine of *tawhīd* as a basic criterion. For example, the Qur'an accuses the Arab pagans of acknowledging idols, metaphysical beings or their self-interests as *ilāh* or a supreme power besides Allah, and consequently of associating them with Allah. Likewise, the Qur'an criticizes the Jews and Christians for accepting Uzayr (Ezra) or Jesus as "the Son of God" in the context of supreme power, and condemns the doctrine of the Trinity.[26] Again the Qur'an disapproves of the attitude of *ahl al-kitāb* taking "their rabbis and monks as lords besides Allah, as well as the Messiah, son of Mary," and states that in fact they are commanded to worship none but one *ilāh*, Allah being the only *ilāh* and above what they associate with him.[27] Another verse also condemns the Christians for their acceptance of Jesus and Mary as *ilāh* besides Allah, and reminds that Jesus delivered the message of worshipping God, the only Lord.[28]

Moreover, the Qur'an emphasizes the doctrine of *tawhīd* in its call for dialogue with other believing systems and non-Muslims. It invites both *ahl al-kitāb* and others to accept that Allah is the only *ilāh* and *rabb* (the only supreme power and decisive factor in human life), and consequently not to associate anyone (or anything) else with him. A remarkable expression of the Qur'an which clearly reflects this call to *ahl al-kitāb* is:

> Say: "O people of the book, come to an equitable word between you and us, that we worship none but Allah, do not associate anything with Him and do not set up others as lords besides Allah." If they turn their backs, say: "Bear witness that we are Muslims."[29]

In another chapter of the Qur'an, after mentioning biblical persons it says, "this, your community is indeed a single community and I am your Lord; so worship me."[30] Likewise the Qur'an explains to the Jews and Christians, who argued that Abraham belonged to their religious tradition, that Abraham was neither a Jew, nor a Christian, nor one of those who associate anything with God, but a *hanīf* and a person who submitted himself to Allah. Hence, referring to Abraham's strict monotheist (*muwahhid*) identity, the Qur'an calls *ahl al-kitāb* to follow the example of Abraham.

As a concluding remark, Islam offers the doctrine of *tawhīd* to all humanity as a criterion of truth. Against the negative influence of hegemonic powers and ideological paradigms on religion, this doctrine can be used by the believing systems, or at least by so-called Abrahamic religions, as a starting point and a base in interfaith relations.

NOTES

1. N. Smart, *The Religious Experience of Mankind* (New York: Collins, 1969), p. 11.
2. See A.D. Foster, "Current Inter-religious Dialogue", M.D. Bryant and F. Flinn (eds.), *Inter-religious Dialogue: Voices from a New Frontier* (New York: Paragon House 1989), p. 47.
3. See H. Küng, "Christianity and World Religions: Dialogue with Islam," L. Swidler (ed.), *Toward a Universal Theology of Religion* (New York: Orbis Books, 1987), p. 193.
4. E. Mortimer, *Faith and Power: The Politics of Islam* (London: Faber and Faber, 1982), p. 33.
5. Although there are some differences between the pluralistic views, they are generally based upon two arguments: (1) Religious traditions appearing within the human cultures in the historical process are the human answers to truth/reality, and (2) all religions can (or may) lead their believers into the truth/reality, but truth/reality is not restricted to any religious tradition.
6. For example, J. Hick, in one of his recent articles, made the conviction "the world going into uniqueness" (tekliğe doğru giden dünya) the basis for his pluralistic arguments. It is also notable that he tries to explain some basic concepts of Christianity like "son of God," "incarnation" etc. metaphorically in order to justify his pluralistic understanding of reality/truth. See Hick, J., "Hıristiyanların İsa'yı Algılama Biçimi ve Bunun İslam'ın Anlayışıyla Karşılaştırılması," *İslâmiyât*, III: 4, 2000, pp. 75–85. Also see E.H. Cousins, "Inter-religious Dialogue: The Spiritual Journey of Our Time," M.D. Bryant and F. Flinn (eds.), *Inter-religious Dialogue: Voices from a New Frontier* (New York: Paragon House, 1989), pp. 5–7.
7. See P. Mojzes, "The What and How of Dialogue," M.D. Bryant and F. Flinn (eds.), *Inter-religious Dialogue: Voices from a New Frontier* (New York: Paragon House, 1989), pp. 201, 205.
8. Al 'Imran [3]:19, 83; al-Ma'ida [5]):3.
9. Al 'Imran [3]:83; al-Tawba [9]:33; al-Saff [61]:9; al-Fath [48]:28.
10. Al-Barqara [2]:130–133; Al 'Imran [3]:67, 52; al-Hajj [22]:78.
11. "We have revealed to you the Book in truth, conforming the scriptures that preceded it and superseded it. Judge between them, then, according to what Allah has revealed, and do not follow their illusory desires, diverging from what came to you of the Truth. To each of you, we have laid down an ordinance and a clear path; and had Allah pleased, He would have made you one nation, but (He wanted) to test you concerning what He gave to you. Be, then, forward in good deeds. To Allah is the ultimate return of all of you, that He may instruct you regarding that on which you differed" (al-Ma'ida [5]:48). "Had Allah wished, He would have made them a single

nation . . ." al-Shura [42]:8. Also see al-Baqara [2]:253; al-Nahl [16]:9, 93; Hud [11]:118.

12. "Had Allah pleased, He would surely have led them all to guidance; so do not be one of the ignorant." Al-An'am [6]:35. Also see al-An'am [6]:107, 112, 137, 149.

13. "Had your Lord willed, everyone on earth would have believed. Will you then compel people to become believers?" Yunus [10]:99.

14. Al-Baqara [2]:256; al-Zalzala [99]: 6–8.

15. "Say: 'O people, the truth has come to you from your Lord; whoever is well-guided is only to his own advantage, and whoever goes astray goes astray only to his disadvantage, and I am not a guardian over you" Yunus [10]:108. "Neither the Jews nor the Christians will be pleased with you until you follow their religion. Say: 'Allah's guidance is the (only) guidance.' And were you to follow their desires after the Knowledge that came down to you, you will have no guardian or helper (to save you) from Allah" (Al-Baqara [2]:120). Also see al-Baqara [2]:147; Al 'Imran [3]: 85–86; al-Saffat [37]:7–9; al-Isra' [17]:81; al-Anbiya' [21]:18; al-Nisa [4]:170; al-Tawba [9]:29, 33; Yunus [10]:94; Luqman [31]:30; Saba' [34]:49–50; al-'Ankabut [29]:52.

16. Al-Hajj [22]:40.

17. Al-Ma'ida [5]:81–83; al-Tawba [9]:97–99; Al 'Imran [3]:75, 110, 113–114, 199; al-Nisa [4]:162.

18. See al-Dhāriyat [51]:56; al-Isrā' [17]:23, 43; al-Nisā [4]:36; An'am [6]:151; Al 'Imrān [3]:2, 18; al-Baqara [2]:117, 163, 255.

19. I.R. Faruki, *Tevhid*, tr. D. Yardım and L. Boyacı (İstanbul: (İnsan, 1995), p. 27.

20. Al-Furqān 43; al-Jāthiya 23.

21. Al-Dhāriya 56; al-Isrā' 23.

22. See, for example, al-A'raf [11]: 59, 65, 73, 85, 104–105; Hûd [7]: 25–28, 50, 61, 84.

23. "We have sent forth to every nation a messenger saying: 'Worship Allah and avoid taghut (anybody or anything against God). . . ." al-Nahl [16]: 36. Also see al-Isrā' [17]: 15.

24. Al-Anbiyā' [21]: 22; al-Mu'minûn [23]: 91.

25. See Faruki, op.cit, p. 59–60.

26. Al-Tawba [9]: 30; al-Nisā [4]: 171; al-Mā'ida [5]: 72–73.

27. Al-Tawba [9]: 31.

28. Al-Mā'ida [5]: 116–117. Regarding this verse, some western scholars maintain that Mary, Jesus's mother, is seen in the Qur'an as one of the Trinity, a misjudgement of the Christian belief, and states that this idea probably comes from the obscure Collyridians before Muhammed. See Watt, W.M., *Muslim-Christian Encounters: Perceptions and Misperceptions* (London: Routledge 1991), p. 23; idem, *Muhammad's Mecca: History in the Qur"an* (Edinburgh University Press, 1988), pp. 2, 45. However, in this verse it should be noticed that the Qur'an does not say that the Christians accept Mary as one of the Trinity, but emphasises that they accept her as *ilāh*, a supreme power whom they venerate.

29. Al 'Imran [3]: 64.

30. Al-Anbiyā' [21]: 92.

Chapter Eleven

WISDOM AS AN INTER-RELIGIOUS CONCEPT FOR PEACE

Cafer Sadik Yaran
Faculty of Theology
University of Istanbul
Istanbul, Turkey

As narrated in the Old Testament, a wise king in Jerusalem, who applied his mind "to seek and to search out by wisdom all that is done under heaven," complains as follows: "Again I saw all the oppressions that are practiced under the sun. Look, the tears of the oppressed—with no one to comfort them!" (Ecc. 4:1).

How many people can claim that this observation and judgment of thousands of years ago is not valid for the present situation of the world? Similar tortures and tears, resembling evils and sufferings go on today as in the past; and new kinds of evil have been added to the old ones and their effects have now been globalized. In the age of knowledge and globalization in which we live, our need of world peace is more urgent than ever, and our responsibility for it is greater than that of our ancestors.

THE IMPORTANCE OF INTER-RELIGIOUS DIALOGUE FOR WORLD PEACE

It is obvious that the global problems of the world require great efforts by global institutions rather than just local and limited endeavors, and religion is of course one of the greatest institutions in the world both historically and geographically. Consequently, there is a direct relationship between world peace

135

and religion. The great world religions believe that striving for world peace is their duty to God and fellow human beings, and that world peace is also useful for their own institutional interests. For in a more peaceful world, it would be religiously easier to answer the historical problem of evil put forth by atheist or skeptical people.

There are various aims of inter-religious dialogue. One of the most important of these aims is the one directed towards inter-religious cooperation for the sake of world peace and the greater good of human beings. The concept of dialogue is sometimes misunderstood and misused by its critics. However, this should not be considered a reason to oppose the development of a sincere and serious inter-religious dialogue. The world desperately needs peace, and the religions certainly have great possibilities to contribute toward peace, especially in cooperation with each other.

THE PRIORITY OF COMMON GROUND
FOR CONSTRUCTIVE DIALOGUE

If world religions really want to contribute to world peace, they must first of all attain a better situation of peace and amity among themselves. In order to reach this goal, they must emphasize the common ground or similar points found in their oral or written encounters, rather than the differences which were emphasized for ages and often caused useless polemic and created feelings of exclusiveness and hostility. In this new era of history, as opposed to the pattern of historical relationships, common and similar concepts must be sought, and they must be given precedence for the sake of dialogue and cooperation.

For example, if there were a common concept or value shared and respected among all the major religions, it would be an appropriate and important concept for beginning and developing constructive dialogue. Moreover, if this concept or value were common and respected in philosophy and science, as well as among the religions, then it would be even more significant. Such respect would mean that this concept or value was truly one of the global concepts and values that is so rarely found. Furthermore, if this concept or value were also a dialogical and peaceful one, then it would be priceless for not only an inter-religious, but also an inter-disciplinary dialogue for the sake of world peace.

Is there such a global and well respected concept or value shared among religions, philosophy and science? Yes, there is. The concept and value of "wisdom" (*hikma*) possesses all of the qualities mentioned above.

WISDOM AS AN INTER-RELIGIOUS
AND INTER-DISCIPLINARY COMMON CONCEPT

According to the *Encyclopaedia of Religion and Ethics*,

> Wisdom may be defined as the direct, practical insight into the meaning and pur-
> pose of things that comes to shrewd, penetrating, and observant minds, from their
> own experience of life, and their daily commerce with the world. It is the fruit not
> so much of speculation as of native sagacity and wit. Consequently, while philoso-
> phy appeals only to the intellectual *élites*, wisdom appeals to all who are interested
> in life and have understanding enough to appreciate a word of truth well spoken.[1]

A different encyclopedic definition reads, "Wisdom was originally a practical
matter, namely 'insight' into certain connections existing in human life and in the
world and modes of behavior derived from this insight and put into the service
of instruction and education."[2] According to the definition of Ibn Sina, one of the
greatest Muslim philosophers, "Wisdom (*hikma*) is the passage of the soul of
man to the perfection possible for him within the two bounds of science and action."[3] It includes, on the one hand, justice, and, on the other, a perfecting of the
reasoning soul. It also comprises theoretical and practical intelligibly.

Wisdom is a common intellectual concept and a cardinal moral value in all the
major religions and in philosophy. For example, according to the Qur'an, being
a good human is closely connected to the amount of wisdom one has: "He
granteth wisdom to whom He pleaseth; And he to whom wisdom is granted re-
ceiveth indeed a benefit overflowing; But none will receive admonition but men
of understanding" (al-Baqara [2]:269). In terms of the Bible, "wisdom excels
folly as light excels darkness" (Ecc. 2:13). In Christian sacred texts, people who
lack wisdom are advised to ask for it from God: "If any of you is lacking in wisdom, ask God, who gives to all generously and ungrudgingly, and it will be
given you" (Jas. 1:5). There is no need to say that in Eastern religions, too, wisdom is regarded as extremely important. It is even difficult to distinguish Indian
wisdom from philosophy, and philosophy in turn from religion; each shares in
the character of the other.[4] It is also worth mentioning in this context that various moral qualities singled out by the classical writers are reduced by Confucius
to the five cardinal virtues, and one of them is wisdom.[5]

In this case some would say: If religion can be broadly conceived as a way of
coping, theoretically and practically, with the problems of the world, nature, and
society, then wisdom is one part of this effort. In fact, wisdom and the various
contents of the religions have historically been closely connected. For example,
in many religions wisdom is an attribute of the divinities; in monotheistic religions it is an attribute of the supreme God. Wisdom was regarded as an area of

religious tradition and derived its authority from its relation to particular gods or God or religious concepts of world order. In this form, wisdom contributed to the development of theological thought and religious morality.[6]

Not only for religion, but also for philosophy, wisdom is among the basic concepts and cardinal virtues. For Socrates, God alone was wise; and the human who claimed actual possession of wisdom was guilty of presumption, if not blasphemy. Taking up a term already used by Pythagoras, he described himself as "a lover of Wisdom." Plato built up his majestic system of ethical idealism, with its four cardinal virtues—wisdom, courage, temperance, and justice. Of these, wisdom is the highest phase of virtue, for it inspires and regulates the whole inner life. A distinction vaguely apprehended by Plato was sharply drawn by Aristotle. Practical wisdom, prudence, or good sense deals with matters of ordinary human interest; speculative wisdom, which is wisdom *par excellence*, with the first principles of things. The former enables a person to apply the right rule to every line of activity, whether professional, civic, or strictly moral; the latter leads, by a union of science and intuitive apprehension, to a knowledge of those things which are most precious in their nature.[7]

Wisdom is also related to science, as well as, to religions and philosophy. According to some people, this relationship has tended to increase recently. As Jean Gebser points out, "people in general are still under the impression that the West lays particular emphasis on the rational function. During the last decades, however, the way was prepared for a decisive change. . . . Surprisingly enough, it is rational science which has disclosed spirituality anew to the West."[8] For Gebser, the spiritual dimension under discussion "does not manifest itself only in nuclear physics. It is also being attained in all the other sciences; biology, psychology, even the study of history and law are examples. In the West, in all branches of learning there are references to the spiritual dimension which, as such, is a characteristic of the new [integral] consciousness."[9] Integration here means "the inclusion of these factors which enable us to gain awareness of a thing in its totality. As applied to modern science it often means the inclusion of the spiritual dimension."[10]

WISDOM AND DIALOGUE: A HISTORICAL AND LEGITIMATE DOOR OPEN TO THE 'OTHER'

Wisdom is one of the most historical and religiously legitimate doors open to the 'other' (religions, cultures, disciplines, etc.). Indeed, the international context of biblical wisdom is already suggested by the claim in *1 Kings* 4: 29, 30, 34 that Solomon's wisdom surpassed that of all the peoples of the East and Egypt:

God gave Solomon very great wisdom, discernment, and breadth of understanding as vast as the sand on the seashore, so that Solomon's wisdom
surpassed the wisdom of all the people of the east, and all the wisdom of Egypt.
. . . People came from all the nations to hear the wisdom of Solomon; they came
from all the kings of the earth who had heard of his wisdom.

Especially from the Islamic perspective, wisdom (*hikma*) seems to be the
most historical and Islamically legitimate door of dialogue with other people.
There is a well-known tradition attributed to the Prophet Muhammad in this
very context. In the tradition, he says that "Wisdom is the lost [property] of
the believer; wherever he finds it, he is the one who deserves to have it
most."[11] It is understood from this tradition that wisdom for a Muslim is not
restricted to the Qur'an and the traditions of the Prophet. There is wisdom in
other places and people whatever religion they have (or even if they do not
have any). Accordingly, to engage in dialogue with the other for the sake of
wisdom seems to be the right and even duty of a Muslim believer.

WISDOM AND PEACEFULNESS:
ALTRUISM AND MODERATION IN THE WISDOM ETHICS

One of the characteristic features of wisdom is its quality of peacefulness.
Wisdom is a peaceful value and all wise people are peace-loving individuals.
It is said concerning the general characteristics of wise people, "Since order
in society, like cosmic order, is divinely ordained, the wise individual is not
disruptive of society."[12] The relationship between wisdom and peacefulness
is openly mentioned in the New Testament: "But the wisdom from above is
first pure, then peaceable, gentle, willing to yield, full of mercy and good
fruits, without a trace of partiality or hypocrisy" (Jas. 3:17).

Peacefulness of the wise is related to their understanding of morality as
well as their beliefs. Two of the most basic and common principles of wise
people's moral behavior seems to be altruism (consideration for others and
love of brother or neighbor) and moderation (the avoidance of extremes).

For example, in Indian wisdom literature, it is written in the context of altruism that "A man of truest wisdom will resign his wealth, and even his life,
for good of others."[13] It is also advised as follows:

To injure none, by thought or word or deed,
    To give to others, and be kind to all-
    This is the constant duty of the good.[14]

There are a lot of recommendations on moderation in various religious and
philosophical wisdom literature. For instance, in the biblical wisdom literature,

humans are advised to follow a path of moderation, to be neither overly righteous nor excessively wicked: "Do not be too righteous, and do not act too wise;
why should you destroy yourself? Do not be too wicked, and do not be a fool;
why should you die before your time?" (Ecc.7: 16,17). In the Qur'an, moderation is also recommended in relation to wisdom, and said that "Make not thy
hand tied (like a niggard's) to thy neck, nor stretch it forth to its utmost reach,
. . . These are among the (precepts of) wisdom, which thy Lord has revealed to
thee" (al-Isra' [17]:29,39). In the wisdom of China too, "We are reminded of the
Greeks when we find wisdom consisting in the avoidance of extremes and the
following of the mean."[15]

Consequently, we have seen that wisdom is an inter-religious, inter-
disciplinary and international global concept and value. It is also a dialogical
and particularly peaceable value. With these characteristic features, it is a
priceless human asset for dialogue and cooperation. It can help humanity to
cope with the problems of the world, and even to reach a more peaceful and
improved condition.

CONCLUDING REMARKS:
THE NEED FOR THE REVIVAL OF WISDOM

Despite all this, it is not possible to say that people always know the value of
wisdom within their own religious and cultural heritages. It may perhaps be
claimed that wisdom has fallen into a crisis, in recent ages, all over the world.
The basic features of wisdom, such as moderation rather than immoderation,
integral consciousness rather than unilateral thought, and altruism rather than
egoism have not been maintained properly in present days. Religious scholars or sages often stressed dogmatism or mysticism excessively and exclusively, and philosophers in turn stressed rationalism and criticism, and scientists stressed empiricism and reductionism. Wisdom seems to be sacrificed
particularly to over-specialization, as well as to other causes. In the end, the
number of sages, wise philosophers and scientists has begun to decrease
among the people of the world. Subsequently, the doors of wisdom that were
open to one another will be locked; and the feelings of alienation and hostility will increase. Consequently, in a world where the number of wise people
becomes less, the number of places which are in peace and harmony will become less.

It seems to me that one of the significant ways to increase dialogue and to
attain world peace is to rescue wisdom from the crisis into which it has fallen
for so long – to revive the concept and value of wisdom, to increase the number of wise people (wise scholars, philosophers, scientists, politicians, econ-

omists, laypersons, etc.) everywhere, and to unlock and open the historical doors of wisdom to each other widely. Human beings (particularly in the West) have seen many different ages in recent centuries, such as the Age of Reason, the Age of Enlightenment, the Age of Science, and now the Age of Knowledge; but none of them seem to have brought to all human beings knowledge, peace, virtue and happiness. Therefore, I hope that, in relying on sincere and wise efforts of inter-religious and inter-disciplinary dialogue, that after the current Age of Knowledge, there would come an "Age of Wisdom" in which knowledge joins together with peace and virtue and is crowned by happiness for as many people as possible all over the world.

NOTES

1. A.R. Gordon, "Wisdom," *Encyclopaedia of Religion and Ethics*, ed. James Hastings, Vol. XII (Edinburgh: T.&T. Clark, 1921), p.742.

2. Kurt Rudolph, "Wisdom," *The Encyclopedia of Religion*, ed. Mircea Eliade, Vol. 15 (New York: MacMillan Publishing Company, 1987), p. 393.

3. A. M. Goichon, "Hikma," *The Encyclopedia of Islam*, New Edition, Vol. III, ed. by B. Lewis *et al* (Leiden: E.J. Brill, 1979).

4. Rudolph, p. 399.

5. Gordon, p. 744.

6. Rudolph, p. 393.

7. Gordon, p. 745.

8. Jean Gebser, "The Trend Towards Integration in Modern Sciences and Its Counterpart in the Ancient Wisdom," in *Eastern Wisdom and Western Thought: A Comparative Study in the Modern Philosophy of Religion*, by P.J. Saher (London: George Allen and Unwin, 1969), p. 9.

9. Gebser, p. 13.

10. Gebser, p. 9.

11. Ibn Mace, *Sünen* (Beirut, 1952), Zühd 15; Tirmizi, Câmius'sahih (Sünenü't-tir 1. izi) (İstanbul: 1992), Ilm, p. 19.

12. Rudolf, p. 403.

13. Gordon, p. 744.

14. Ibid.

15. Rudolf, p. 400.

Chapter Twelve

SOME REMARKS ON THE AUTHORITY OF SACRED TEXTS AND VIOLENCE

Burhanettin Tatar
Ondokoz Mayis University
Samsun, Turkey

INTRODUCTION

Why is human nature inclined to violence? Is violence a historical dimension of humanity being-in-the-world or an inherent part of human nature? Obviously, these questions take us toward a metaphysical domain if they are investigated from the horizon opened up by the questions themselves. What makes them open questions is the plurality and potentiality of languages within which we live. When these questions are investigated from the horizon opened up by the language we employ, they become meaningful and fruitful, helping us get to the heart of the matter, which is found at the point of fusion between language and violence. It is interesting to me to look at the qur'anic verses which talk about Adam's language and Adam's position with regard to his being and other creatures. We get the impression from the relevant qur'anic verses that the first violent action of Adam toward himself and God's command, which limited his condition in the Garden, appears after his learning the language and the names of the creatures. With this impression, we should ask the question—what is the relationship between language and violence?

We know that violence is something that can happen when a possibility of access to being something else is present. Violence has the character of 'going-beyond-the-limit-of.' Said differently, violence takes place when the limits and borders of a legitimate domain are broken down by an alien power, and this domain is transformed into a new condition according to the desire of the alien power. This analysis shows us that what makes violence possible is the possibility of accessing other domains. At this point, it is becoming clear that the only possibility of accessing other domains is provided by language itself. Language lets us get new connections and penetration into other beings and impose our own plans and ideas upon them. Hence language does not function only to bring other things to our consciousness but also allows us to re-form them according to our capacity to form new ideas concerning them.

Therefore, language provides the possibility of violence. Indeed, this is not the mere function of language, but it provides us with the consciousness of violence, which is possible via language. Hence language becomes the possibility of both violence and non-violence as long as the consciousness of violence becomes the basis of preventing and stopping violence. This simple but basic argument leads us to make another argument that only human beings act violently within the domain opened by the language which they employ. Animals cannot act violently simply because they are not conscious of violence and a language of violence.

The relationship between language and violence seems to me to be very perplexing, because language becomes silent when violence speaks and violence becomes silent when language speaks. In other words, when language becomes the language of violence and is spoken in the name of violence, language itself becomes a mere structure of signs that represent the unjustified oppressing and dominating action of a people. When language becomes the language of violence, it is transformed into a sign and representation of political and economical interests, as the critique of ideology by Jurgen Habermas has already pointed out. Hence when language provides the possibility of violence, it becomes something else—that is, an instrument for the sake of violence. When language provides the possibility of non-violence, it becomes a source of power and resistance against violence. One of the possibilities of the language of non-violence is to de-structure and de-construct the language of violence. A language movement against another language movement shows us clearly that language itself is able to take us beyond the language of violence.

The diametrical opposition between the language of violence and the language of non-violence turns us toward another key notion, namely, text. Text is a part of language. In this sense, text speaks about a topic which is relevant to the human world of meaning. We learn from hermeneutics and the philosophy of language that language does not only speak "about a topic" which is part of the human world of meaning, but it also "constructs" it through text. This constructing power also has the ability to create different worlds. Human beings live within different worldviews, at the center of which an authoritative text functions. Viewed from this point, most violent actions can be regarded as the result of possible effects of an authoritative text. In other words, an authoritative text provides its readers and interpreters with different possible ways of living. Even if violence is not suggested by this text directly as a goal, a violent action can be chosen by the interpreter as a means toward realization of a possible way of living. What about the relationship between the authoritative sacred texts and violence?

-I-

Sacred texts cannot be authoritative in isolation from communities who perceive them to be sacred or holy. Hence the problem of the authority of the sacred texts should be taken into consideration primarily in terms of the historical interactions between these kinds of texts and their communities. This paper first aims to deal with these historical interactions within the context of the politics of violence, which is (1) grounded on the authority of the sacred texts, and (2) applied to the sacred texts themselves. Secondly, the question of whether the authority of sacred texts can be secured from all kinds of politics of violence will be discussed.

In the history of Islam, the bloody events which arose after the assassination of the early caliphs Umar, Uthman, Ali and the subsequent political regimes, which were also the outcomes of bloody violence, as well as the historical conflicts between Muslims and people of other faiths, have usually been related to the historical authority of the Qur'an. Interestingly enough, a paradox has always existed in the fact that conflicting groups are accustomed to resorting to the authority of the sacred texts in order to justify their arguments when the sacred texts were intended to control natural violence in human beings by purifying their motives ethically and psychologically. We can see the clearest reflection of this paradoxical situation when we notice a politic of violence arising with reference to the authority of the sacred texts, which is in fact a politic of violence that is being exerted on the sacred texts themselves. For instance, all kinds of tyrannical regimes and esoteric interpretations in Islam are different politics of violence being applied to its sacred texts.

Doubtless, one can make a distinction between the different politics of violence that are applied to the sacred texts. For instance the politics of violence to which a tyrannical regime resorts differs, in terms of goal and means, from the politics of violence that a mystical (esoteric) interpretation brings into play with regard to the sacred texts. The former aims at legitimating the violence it uses toward society, while the latter strives to resist the violence of a political regime or a radical religious community. Moreover, there is a difference between a mystical (esoteric) interpretation which utilizes a politic of violence at the level of anti-rational discourse so as to justify itself and a philosophical interpretation which exercises a politic of violence on the sacred texts at the level of logical and rational discourse.

After getting in intellectual touch with the Western world, Islamic thought welcomed different politics of violence, such as 'historical criticism' and 'deconstructionism' which were developed within the dynamics of Western culture.

Historical criticism is a method of reducing the world of meaning in a historical text to the world of meaning behind the text (i.e., to the original historical context of the text). In its reductionist effort, historical criticism does violence to the dynamic world of meaning because the text has constantly changing situations. In other words, it forces the text to return to its original historical context by disregarding its own historical life.

Deconstructionism presupposes that the identity (internal coherence) of a historic text is only an ideological illusion. Deconstructionists claim that when one uncovers the basic structures of the text, one will notice that the so-called identity (internal coherence) of the text is merely a mask hiding the conflicting structures.

The politic of violence called deconstruction has been exerted not only on the written texts but also on some nations, formed out of different ethnic communities. Deconstruction played a significant role in the destruction of the former Soviet Union and Yugoslavia.

Moreover, we can notice within the context of inter-religious dialogue traces of the politics of violence within the inclusivist, exclusivist and pluralist discourses regarding the sacred texts. For instance, in the inclusivist discourse, all other sacred texts are interpreted as historical and regional texts although claiming to be universal, and their historical and regional boundaries are expected to dissolve within the course of time.

As to the exclusivist discourse, the boundaries between the sacred texts are drawn mostly by the interpretive communities and are considerably ideological. The expression 'ideological boundaries' means that most of the interpretive communities perceive the boundaries of their interpretation to be the boundaries of the textual meaning and hence assume their ideas to be the center (core) of the meaning of the text. These so-called ideological boundaries function as the basis of justifying some economical, political and religious conflicts. These boundaries are largely determined by historical conditions. In Islamic history, the absence of conclusive agreement between the legal, political, theological, mystical, philosophical and economic approaches to the boundaries between sacred texts is not an accidental event.

Within the pluralist discourses, of which John Hick's approach seems to be most representative, sacred texts are reduced to the level of the historical responses of the religious communities toward a universal Truth (Reality). In claiming this, pluralist discourse tacitly assumes a meta-discourse that determines the real boundaries of the sacred texts and hence desires to act as a supreme judge between them. We observe within this kind of pluralist discourse a typical reflection of modernist reason, which perceives itself to be the source of validation for religious symbols and proclamation.

The politics of violence, which are grounded on the authority of sacred texts or are applied to them, have given rise to many bloody conflicts and to persecution. The politics of violence applied to the sacred texts over a long period of time in the Western and Islamic worlds. This situation causes not only the dissolution of religious symbols, which enliven ethical and religious life, but also the diminishment of historical resistance of societies against globalization.

-II-

In the face of this situation, one of the significant questions which should concern us is: How is it possible to interpret the historical authority of the sacred texts in a way that does not cause sacred texts to be used to rationalize the politics of violence or to be subject to the violence? We will deal with this question with reference to the historical manifestations of the authority of the qur'anic text.

The Qur'an declared the basic notions and symbols of pagan belief to be deprived of reality and criticized the pagan tradition as the unreal basis of these notions and symbols. It became a center of meaning and communication between some people, leading them to form an Islamic community. In this context, some distinctions can be made between the historical functions of different forms of the qur'anic text within Islamic societies. For instance, the Qur'an functioned as a central authority, which was concretized within time and space by turning toward immediate situations in the forms of verbal and actual texts via the life of the Prophet Muhammad. It gained its absolute autonomy after it was written down in the form of a book. Memorizing it does not merely aim at securing its written form from all kinds of distortion, but is also a sign of fidelity to its authority and of internalizing it so that it reaches its verbal and actual being whenever it is intended to. The historical continuity of its interpretations up to the present days indicates that its authority has been resorted to in constantly changing situations. From this perspective, the Qur'an appears to be the authority functioning as a dynamic center of meaning and communication by renewing itself constantly.

The Qur'an has established its general authority as a dynamic center of meaning and communication in the form of a symbolic text. Here the expression 'symbolic text' is not to be taken to mean that it represents some reality or refers to some truth. Rather, it is a symbolic text, which makes it possible for people believing it to recognize and understand each other in a distinct way. We take the word 'symbol' (*sumbolon*) in its original meaning. In ancient Greek, *sumbolon* meant a token, an insignia, or a means of identification by which parties, allies, guests and hosts, and other kinds of partners could identify each other. Each partner was supposed to keep a part of a token so that when he/she met other partners his/her part would form a meaningful, coherent whole with the other parts. For that reason, in its original meaning, the word 'symbol' refers to a coherent whole that can be formed only when the partners are in peaceful relation with each other.

The Qur'an is a symbolic text in the sense of being a central authority, which has made it possible for a significant part of the world to gain a common meaning under the name of Islam. In the history of Islam, the authority of verbal, written, mental and actual forms of qur'anic text, as God's command, has been perceived mostly in the form of vertical understanding. However, the authority of its symbolic text has required horizontal understanding, since it has made it possible for some people to recognize and understand each other as Muslims.

The expression 'the form of vertical understanding' indicates the understanding of beings, discourses and meanings within a hierarchical value system descending from higher to lower. Classical Islamic thought has generally been formed within this vertical understanding, which is of metaphysical character. For instance, the qur'anic discourse was perceived within the hierarchical value system descending from the higher to the lower such as binding duty (*fard*), incumbent obligation (*vacib*), licit (*mandub*), legitimate (*mubah*); or firm (*muhkam*), similar (*mutashabih*); or command (*amr*), narrative (*habar*); or legal (*halal*), forbidden (*haram*). The classification of the qur'anic meanings by Islamic philosophers as rationally and logically demonstrational (*burhani*), dialectical (*jadali*) and metaphorical (*hatabi, majazi*) is based on the form of vertical understanding. No doubt, understanding the qur'anic discourse within the form of vertical understanding has affected the self-perceptions of Muslim communities and the organization of sciences in the age of classical Islam. From the political point of view, the communities were perceived within a hierarchical value system descending from the higher to the lower such as caliph, judges (*fukaha*), scholars (*ulama*), ordinary people; from the religious viewpoint, religious leader (*imam*), vice-regent (*naib*), saints (*wali*), exoteric scholars, ordinary people. Each scientific branch has been classified and evaluated within the general category of religious and worldly sciences.

The expression 'the form of horizontal understanding' refers to understanding the relation between beings, discourses and meanings within the context of common historical problems and issues. The form of horizontal understanding is of historical character and hence differs from the form of vertical understanding, which is of metaphysical character. In the form of horizontal understanding, the value of a being, text, or interpretation is determined in terms of its function and participation in the solution of a historical problem. For that reason, it is different from the form of vertical understanding, which has a metaphysical value system as its basis. It assumes that the value of a being, text, and interpretation is determined historically and temporally simply because they are of a dynamic and temporal nature and character.

Today the people who perceive the authority of the qur'anic text mostly within the form of vertical understanding are called 'conservative traditionalists' and those who perceive it mostly within the form of horizontal understanding are named 'liberal modernists.' In my opinion, each form of understanding has its own problems with regard to the authority of the Qur'an. Yet, the problem, which is common for both forms, is that they do not take the symbolic text of the Qur'an as the basis of understanding its other textual forms. If the authority of the Qur'an is to be secured from all kinds of politics of violence, its symbolic text must be taken as the basis of understanding its other textual forms. This is simply because of the historical fact that when the authority of a sacred text fails to lead people to mutual understanding, its other textual forms can easily be taken to be the basis of (and subject to) the politics of violence.

One can notice that the authority of the sacred texts is here taken to be an emancipating communication (meaning) center between human beings. Surely, there is a very close relationship between the notion of emancipation and that of mutual understanding and communication. No genuine emancipation is possible if every human being is supposed to stay within a specific confinement and limitations. Emancipation is a process that happens in proportion to the degree to which people participate in the production of something good for humanity, and is self-renewing within the communicative situation and where mutual understanding is concretized. Those who are not allowed (or able) to renew themselves and participate to produce something good for humanity are forced to stay within the limits determined by others and to submit to their politics of violence.

For that reason, when the authority of sacred texts is taken as the basis of mutual understanding and communication, the possibility of having a dynamic interaction and of participating to produce something good can arise by overcoming the ideological limitations. Is it not the authority of sacred texts, as the basis of mutual understanding and communication, which forces us today to have a dialogical relation with people of other faiths?

CONCLUSION

If the strivings for inter-religious dialogue are expected to yield world peace, the authority of sacred texts must first be secured from all kinds of politics of violence and function in the form of symbolic texts. As long as the authority of sacred texts can lead its followers to produce something good by strengthening mutual understanding, both among themselves and with the people of other faiths, there can be an emancipating authority. Otherwise, such authority can easily be the source of legitimization behind the politics of violence due to some ideological confinements put on it. As mentioned above, a sacred text that functions as the basis of a politic of violence is already subjected to the same politics of violence. The duty of the people of faith who long for a peaceful world is to secure their sacred texts from this paradoxical situation.

Index